The Best of Jacobean Appliqué

Patricia B. Campbell
& Mimi Ayars, Ph.D.

American Quilter's Society

P. O. Box 3290 • Paducah, KY 42002-3290
e-mail: AQSquilt@apex.net

Located in Paducah, Kentucky, the American Quilter's Society (AQS) is dedicated to promoting the accomplishments of today's quilters. Through its publications and events, AQS strives to honor today's quiltmakers and their work and to inspire future creativity and innovation in quiltmaking.

EDITOR: CHERRY PYRON
BOOK DESIGN: LISA M. CLARK
ILLUSTRATIONS: WHITNEY HOPKINS
COVER DESIGN: MICHAEL BUCKINGHAM
PHOTOGRAPHY: CHARLES R. LYNCH

Library of Congress Cataloging-in-Publication Data

Campbell, Patricia B. (Patricia Boyan), 1941-
    The best of Jacobean appliqué / Patricia B. Campbell & Mimi Ayars.
        p.cm.
    ISBN 1-57432-738-0
        1. Appliqué--Patterns. 2. Quilting--Patterns. 3. Decoration and ornament,
Jacobean. I. Ayars, Mimi. II. Title.

TT779.C35 2000
746.46'041--dc21   00-023157
                                                  CIP

Additional copies of this book may be ordered from the American Quilter's Society, PO Box 3290, Paducah, KY 42002-3290 @ $24.95. Add $2.00 for postage and handling.

Copyright © 2000, Patricia B. Campbell & Mimi Ayars

Dedication

from PAT to
"my appliqué loving friends around the world"

from MIMI to
"my friend, cheerleader, and helpmate of fifty years"

Contents

Section 1

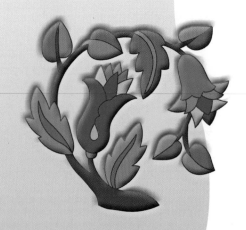

INTRODUCING...

JACOBEAN

Jacobean (pronounced "Jack'-u-bee'-un") derives from Jacobus Britannia Rex, the formal title of seventeenth century English King James I, who succeeded Queen Elizabeth I. He is the king of the King James version of the Bible. During his reign, the colonies at Jamestown and Plymouth were settled. Shakespeare was alive then. Architecture, furniture, literature, entertainment, and embroidery of a distinctive style reflected the times to such an extent that they can be identified today.

Jacobean embroidery differs from other forms of needlework, not by the stitches, but by the thread and the design. The thread, made of soft, slackly twisted, two-ply worsted yarn was worked with a needle on linen. Glorious shading of pastels and bright colors gave dimension to the flora and fauna of not only England but also distant lands. Colors ranged from deep green to contrasting rose, purple, blue, and gold – calming, soothing. It is generally thought the colors were muted, but perhaps it has been time that mellowed them rather than the stitcher.

An air of fantasy and romance permeated the compositions, usually floral or arboreal with deeply notched leaves, undulating vines, intertwined branches and stems, coiling tendrils, and imaginative flowers. Distinguishable characteristics include the Oriental *Tree of Life* with graceful branches and rolling mounds, and the Elizabethan scroll with sweeping stems swirling around flowers, a wavy border, oversized leaves with curled or notched edges, and curved blossoms.

Treasured family pieces of Jacobean embroidery emigrated to the colonies in the possessions of the English colonists. The needlewomen in our country changed the name to *crewel* (spelled a number of different ways), and the designs were adapted to American taste. These were less busy than the old designs with greater variety and more unadorned background. Realistic designs, reflective of everyday American life, replaced the fantasy ones. There was a lightness, a vitality, a gaiety unlike the English counterpart: a freedom of spirit unique to the new land. Wall and bed hangings were cherished and passed from one generation to the next with great pride. Household items, such as table covers, chair seats, and bedspreads, were decorated with Jacobean stitchery.

Some fine examples of early Jacobean needlework can be seen at Colonial Williamsburg, Virginia; the Henry Ford Museum, Greenfield Village, Dearborn, Michigan; the Shelburne Museum, Vermont; and Winterthur, Delaware.

APPLIQUÉ

The word *appliqué*, taken from the Latin *applicare* meaning *to fasten to*, comes to English via French, adopted *wholecloth* even to the accent mark over the *e*.

Appliqué is probably as old as humanity and seems to be universal. From the Innuits' decorating their skins with other skins to East Indians' attaching mirrors to cotton, from Siberia to Peru, possessions have been embellished with appliqué. Although appliqué can refer to applying any material onto any other material in any manner, it has come to mean, especially to quiltmakers, stitching one fabric piece onto the surface of another fabric piece. In earlier times this technique was called *laid-on* or *patchwork*.

JACOBEAN APPLIQUÉ

A new quilt art form was created when Patricia B. Campbell, retaining the spirit of the antique pieces, began translating old Jacobean embroidery designs into new Jacobean appliqué designs.

The designs are based on classic botanical shapes which have been simplified for appliqué. Focusing on fantasy rather than realism, they are charming and fun to stitch.

Exotica #1, p. 48

Exotica #2, p. 52

Exotica #3, p. 56

Section 2

Gathering Tools & Supplies

TOOLS

SANDPAPER BOARD

If you have never used a sandpaper board and a Styrofoam wall panel, you simply must get acquainted pronto. They will become your best friends.

A sandpaper board can be fancy or simple, purchased or homemade. It keeps the fabric from slipping and prevents distorting the design piece when templates are being traced. Make one by gluing a sheet of fine sandpaper to plywood, a clipboard, or the inside of a file folder. From the first time used, piecers as well as appliquérs will keep this helper close by.

STYROFOAM WALL PANEL

After the design fabric pieces have been cut and positioned on your background fabric block, you will want to look at the arrangement from a distance to check on color, balance, harmony, and contrast. Inexpensive Styrofoam panels, available from the lumber yard, covered with flannel and attached to the wall, are an ideal way to accomplish this. Hanging your blocks on the wall will help you *read* your fabric combinations from across the room. If space is at a premium at your house, make a portable wall panel 4' x 4' (122 cm x 122 cm) and store it when not in use, perhaps in the garage.

Most quiltmakers maintain a collection of basic tools and a supply of basic materials. Check your quilt tool box and your supply closet, using the following list to double check the essentials.

SCISSORS

To maintain the sharpness of your fabric scissors, use them only on fabric, never on paper or plastic. Embroidery scissors are recommended for cutting out the design pieces; scissors for machine appliqué are too heavy. Use craft scissors on plastic and paper; kitchen scissors are heavy and fatigue the hand.

NEEDLES

A small needle makes a small hole in the fabric; a large needle, a large hole. A long needle, called a *milliner's* (#7 Sharps) or *straw*, wobbles, bends, and is hard to control. A gold needle is like a nail. A platinum needle sounds romantic, but those who have indulged in the luxury of one suggest they bend. Save your money for a ring instead.

The smaller the needle the better, because it's stronger and does not bend. Only ⅓ of its length is needed for turning, so why push more through the material? Although the eye is small, the recommended thread is thin. Threading should not be a problem; if it is, a threader is available for fine needles.

You already quilt with a little needle. Why learn to use another size? Try a #12 Between faithfully for a week. If a #12 feels foreign, try a #10. Experiment until you find a size you like. Always stitch with what is comfortable for you, not with what you're told is the right needle. Consider having a number of needles in use, like in quilting, so you have to stop and start less frequently.

THIMBLE

A thimble is protection against puncture wounds from the *blunt* end of the needle. Sore fingers delay stitching, maddening for an avid appliquér. If you have never worn a thimble, persevere for a week. Believe it or not, in that short time you'll learn to wear one with ease.

Exotica #4, p. 60

Exotica #5, p. 64

Exotica #6, p. 68

PINS

Sequin pins, sometimes called appliqué pins, are especially good for holding circles and other small pieces in place until stitching is well started. If there is a choice of length, choose ¾" (2 cm). Avoid those sold in craft shops; they're thick and blunt.

Sashiko pins, also called appliqué pins, are silk pins with glass heads and are very thin and sharp. Use them to pin pieces to the master pattern. They make no holes in the fabric, but they do make holes in fingers. Treat them with respect.

Use quilting pins to help make perfect points, a technique that will be discussed later.

PIN CUSHION

A household with children, animals, and spouses who have magnetic feet needs a pin monitor. In the early days when pins were handmade and expensive, needlewomen had a creative way to keep track of every single one. A design was made in the pin cushion with the pins. When one was missing, the owner knew immediately and looked for it. Consider following their example. Glass headed pins are easier to find when dropped. A strong magnet or a flashlight kept handy for a pin search is helpful.

Old-time needlewomen claimed that a pin cushion stuffed with wool batting or hair kept needles rust free and one made with sand or gravel sharpened them.

PENS

For tracing the patterns in this book onto the master pattern, use a permanent black thin line pen. Avoid using either a grease pencil or a ball point pen; they smear. Use a permanent pen on the plastic templates, if a black edge is desired.

PENCILS

Silver and white pencils show up best on dark fabrics, darker pencils on light fabrics. A mechanical lead pencil keeps its point and lets you draw close to the template. Regular lead pencils dull easily and stitching time is lost trying to keep them sharp. A yellow wax pencil shows up well on dark cloth, but will melt if touched by a hot iron, leaving a yellow mark where you probably won't want one. Check with your quilt shop to see if a yellow water soluble pencil is available. Always test a product before using it on your project, no matter how well recommended it comes.

ERASER

Ideally, you won't have any marks to remove from the fabric. However, here are some suggestions if you do have a stray mark: a clean *rubber finger*; a cotton ball; cotton batting for white or silver pencil; cheap hair spray; a formula of 3 tablespoons alcohol, 1 tablespoon water, and 2 drops of dish detergent. Try every suggestion of this type on a sample of fabric before daring to apply it to your needlework piece.

Speaking of mark removal, don't forget the old and proven method for removing blood: chew a piece of white cotton thread and when well wet with saliva, dab it on the spot. The thread absorbs the blood.

EMERY BOARD

An emery board works well to file any little peaks that result when cutting out plastic templates, particularly circles.

BIAS-MAKING GADGETS

Although bias strips can be made as our grandmothers did, there are wonderful gadgets, available to ease the job, that make beautiful bias pieces in finished widths from ⅛" to ¾" (.3 to 2 cm). Also an attachment is available for most sewing machines.

LIGHT BOX

A light box is required if you plan to mark the master pattern on a dark background. A commercial one is expensive, but you can improvise in one of the following ways: 1. the old-fashioned way of taping the background fabric block over the pattern to a window; 2. using a lamp in a waste basket covered with glass or plastic; 3. pulling apart a leaf table and placing a piece of glass or a plastic desk protector over the opening and a lamp underneath; 4. positioning a lamp under a glass table top.

SUPPLIES

MASTER PATTERN MATERIAL

A number of materials may be used for the master pattern. Choose inexpensive, lightweight, non-woven, non-fusible interfacing; the paper that covers the examining table at a physician's office; or freezer paper.

TEMPLATE MATERIAL

Templates can be made from a number of materials. Clear plastic is ideal because it permits an advantageous placing on the design fabric; you can see exactly how the piece will look when cut out. A pattern on duplicating paper can be laminated and used as a template, but it's opaque.

BATTING

Batting thickness and composition are a personal choice. Since a wall quilt is not for warmth but for show, the batting can be lightweight polyester or cotton.

APPLIQUÉ THREAD

In Jacobean appliqué you want your stitches to be hidden so that the design, rather than the stitch, catches the eye. Machine embroidery thread is best because it's thinner than regular sewing thread and hides well. Avoid polyester thread except for blends because it can cut through the fabric. Rayon comes in beautiful shades and has a sheen, but it untwists. Silk thread curls and is expensive.

QUILTING THREAD

Quilting thread the color of the background fabric keeps the quilting from competing with the appliqué design.

OTHER ESSENTIALS

Two absolute essentials are needed: a good light and a comfortable chair. To stitch well you must see well. Provide yourself with the best light available both day and night. Select a chair that fits your anatomy so that your body and your needle can spend many pleasurable hours together.

NEED TO KNOW

Q. What thread should I use?

A. Cotton for cotton, silk for silk, polyester for polyester.

Q. Where can I find this thread?

A. Some quilt shops. Sewing centers teach embroidery classes, so they carry it more often than quilt shops do.

CHECK LIST
FOR TOOLS & SUPPLIES

_ Sandpaper board
_ Styrofoam wall board
_ Scissors
_ Needles
_ Thimble
_ Pins
_ Pin cushion
_ Pens
_ Pencils
_ Eraser
_ Emery board
_ Bias-making gadgets
_ Light box
_ Master pattern material
_ Template material
_ Batting
_ Appliqué thread
_ Quilting thread

Section 3

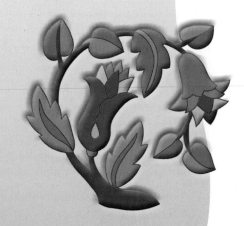

Colors & Fabrics

COLOR

Color anxiety plagues many a quiltmaker. Symptoms include fabric selection jitters, slavish devotion to somebody else's pattern, avoid-a-decision syndrome, never-trust-my-own-judgment mentality, better-safe-than-sorry philosophy.

An active discussion ensued at a recent quilting bee in response to a newcomer's question, "How do you choose the fabric for your quilt?"

"I just tell the clerk what color I want and she picks out the material." ... "I follow the photos in the book." ... "No problem. I love blue so I just buy shades of blue." ... "I go with the coordinates of the fabric company." ... "Trial and error." ... "Whatever's 'in' this year." ... "My friends and I pool our ignorance." (Giggles) ... "Nina's got color sense, so I ask her." ... A chorus of "yeahs."

If you see yourself reflected in these comments, you're going to love making a Jacobean appliqué quilt because you'll have a new freedom you may never have experienced before. You'll break out of the "everything coordinated" mold. You'll use a wide array of colors and prints. You'll try new combinations. You'll no longer follow the leader, but discover you have wings and can fly.

Although a color dictionary names 4,000 colors and it's said there may be 10 million distinguishable colors, the quilt-maker is limited by what's available in textile dyes, what colors are in fashion, and what the manufacturers have decided to produce in fabric. Even so, the possibilities are extensive.

Color is cultural. Look at African Kente cloth, beautiful and expensive. The use of such dominant colors as royal purple and Halloween orange together is not uncommon, yet in American-made cloth this combination is rare. White is worn in our country by brides; in China, by mourners. In Japan light green is for youth; dark green for the aged. In America today blue is for baby boys and pink for baby girls, yet 100 years ago it was the reverse. Many Native Americans express the four points of the compass with color names.

Color affects emotions. Blue and green used together calm; red and yellow excite. Subdued colors like dark purple give a feeling of richness and elegance; bright colors like hot pink express liveliness and gaiety. Dark tones like midnight blue seem sad and moody; light tones like dusty pink, frivolous. Does gray make you sad? And yellow, happy? Red, white, and blue, proud?

Color has invaded our language. When Helen Keller was asked if she could see color, she smiled and said, "Sometimes I see red," and then she added, "sometimes I feel blue."

Color is personal. What is the dominant color in your fabric treasure chest? In your home? Do you like cherry red and chartreuse together? Lemonade yellow and flamingo pink? These combinations set some people's teeth on edge.

There are folks who do seem to have an eye for color, just as some have an ear for music. Harmony and discord are generally associated with music, but apply also to color. The composition, whether consisting of notes or colors, is pleasant or unpleasant, jarring or soothing.

There are at least three languages of color, one from the physics world, one from the field of psychology, and one from artists. Even when these groups use a common term, it may mean different things. For example, they all talk about primary colors, usually naming red, blue, and yellow, but physicists also include green as a primary color.

Exotica #7, p. 72

Exotica #8, p. 76

Exotica #9, p. 80

There are a profusion of color names and a confusion of color terms; no wonder quiltmakers are puzzled. Of course, you don't have to speak the language of color to create a beautiful wallhanging, but let's talk about some of these often intimidating terms so you'll no longer be afraid of them. We'll use the vocabulary of the artist. A little basic knowledge of color will help in your fabric selection.

You probably heard of the color wheel (a circle) in your school days, but a six-pointed star, composed of two equilateral triangles positioned to form an inside hexagon may be easier for quiltmakers to visualize.

Let's designate the points of the first triangle red, blue, and yellow, the *primary* colors (Fig. 1). Primary colors do not involve any other color and all other colors can be produced from combinations of these three colors.

You may recall that mixing two primary colors in equal proportion produces the *secondary* colors: red

and blue make purple; blue and yellow make green; and yellow and red make orange. Let's designate the points of the second triangle purple, green, and orange (Fig. 2). Now the points of the star are red, purple, blue, green, yellow, and orange (Fig. 3).

Mixing any two adjacent *hues* (colors) produces a new hue. If we mix a primary and a secondary color in equal proportion, the combination is expressed as a hyphenated word with the primary color expressed first. Therefore, the points of the hexagon are designated red-purple, blue-purple, blue-green, yellow-green, yellow-orange, and red-orange (Fig. 4). If we alter the proportion of one color to the other, the resulting new color will reflect that difference with the color of the greater amount being stronger. Look at Native American jewelry in which some turquoises are bluish and some are greenish.

Now we have a basic color star (Fig. 5). *Analogous* colors are neighbors. See that red-orange, orange, and yellow-orange reside next door to one another

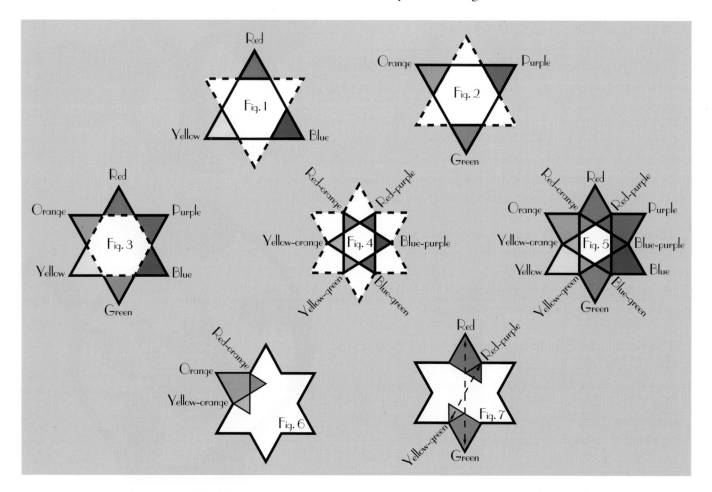

(Fig. 6). *Complementary* colors are directly opposite each other; red and green or red-purple and yellow-green are at the ends of a straight line from point to point (Fig. 7).

Painters generally mix their pigments with a palette knife or brush, but Impressionists like Seurat (who was sometimes called a Pointillist) painted small dots directly onto the canvas, one next to another, letting the viewer's eye mix the dots to achieve the effect he had in mind. If we stand close to a Seurat painting, we see only individual spots of paint; if we stand back, we see the composition. This is what happens with Jacobean appliqué; the colors merge in the eye so we need to stand back five or six feet to see this blending.

CONTRAST

Just as a realtor advises prospective buyers that there are three things to remember when buying property, *location, location, location,* you are advised that there are three things to remember when making a Jacobean appliqué quilt: *contrast, contrast, contrast.*

Contrast is the magic in planning a Jacobean appliqué quilt: different colors (hue), lights and darks (value), high and low brilliance (intensity), accent, warm and cool (temperature), large and small (scale), smooth and rough (texture), and bright and muted (tone). Having too little contrast is like not having enough salt in the soup. When contrasts occur, the result is variety, stimulation, depth, movement, and drama.

Let's explore contrast in terms of *hue, value, intensity, accent, temperature, scale, texture,* and *tone.*

Hue – *color*

Hues glow with contrast and are ho-hum without it. Compare the tulips from Design #5 in the photographs on page 27. Is one tulip more radiant than the other? Contrast makes the difference. Colors that are closely related are boring; those that are *distant cousins* are entertaining.

One color can dominate, but the others need to enhance it. Reds and greens have been the most popular combination for quiltmakers down through the generations. You can't go wrong letting these two colors predominate in your composition, but complementary hues of equal amounts in the same piece of fabric should not be used because the eye in mixing them will perceive one hue – gray.

Use any green with any other green; Mother Nature mixes them all together. A wide variety of greens is always needed, from the mysterious tone of a dense forest to the crystal tint of a shimmering iceberg.

Value – *light and dark*

Value refers to the gradations of *tints* (lights) and *shades* (darks) of a specific color. When white is added to a pure color, it lightens it. For example, white added to red results in pink (tint). The amount of white determines how light it is. Black added to a pure color darkens it; the amount of black determines how dark. For example, black added to red results in cranberry (shade).

The gradations from lightest to darkest are numerous. Fig. 8 on the following page portrays a small range of blues: baby blue, powder blue, and sky blue are tints; cadet blue, denim blue, and navy blue are shades. Pure colors also differ in value; for example, yellow is lighter in value than blue.

Although tint means pure color plus white, *pastel* is the popular term. Although shade means pure color plus black, quiltmakers commonly use shade to refer to all the values of a color from palest to darkest. Mint green, grass green, forest green we call shades of green and forest green, a dark shade of green.

Two shades placed next to each other accentuate their difference, but when a number of different greens appear together, green as such, becomes superior to any one of the individual green fabrics.

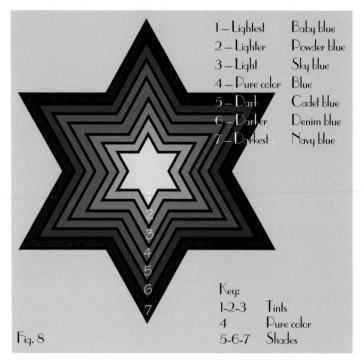

1 – Lightest	Baby blue
2 – Lighter	Powder blue
3 – Light	Sky blue
4 – Pure color	Blue
5 – Dark	Cadet blue
6 – Darker	Denim blue
7 – Darkest	Navy blue

Key:
1-2-3	Tints
4	Pure color
5-6-7	Shades

Fig. 8

Intensity – *high and low*

Intensity refers to the degree of brilliance of a hue. The closer a hue is to the pure color, the higher the intensity and the brighter the hue. For example, royal purple is of higher intensity than lavender.

Two contrasting colors with the same intensity used in equal amounts are like hard rock on a boom box. Two contrasting colors with the same intensity used in unequal amounts is like a polka on an accordion. Some colors are naturally more intense than others; for example, yellow is more intense than blue.

Hue, value, and intensity are interrelated. If you change one, you change the other two. For example, if you change the hue from pure blue to baby blue, now a new hue, you have changed the value (made it lighter) and the intensity (lowered it).

Accent

Accent is accomplished by using only a touch of color, especially one high in intensity – mustard yellow, hot pink, orange – in the same way that a chartreuse scarf gives zest to a navy blue suit. The Amish know this fact well and use icy tints to accent their shades.

A fabric accent will do for your quilt top what a special spice will do for your recipe, but if you over-use a favorite accent color, the purpose of scattered highlights is defeated. Some colors whimper, others scream. Keep the screamers confined to small areas.

Temperature – *warm and cool*

Warm colors (reds, oranges, yellows) advance, excite, stimulate; cool colors (blues, purples, greens) retreat, calm, soothe. The warm colors pull and the cool colors push. Both are needed, each enhancing the other. One shade (or tint) of a color can be warmer or cooler than another shade (or tint) of the same color. For example, traffic-light red is warmer than barn door red. An illusion of depth can be created through the retreat of cool colors and the advance of warm ones.

Scale – *large and small*

Printed fabrics with large patterns and printed fabrics with small patterns arouse interest. The large prints delight the eye and the small ones appeal to the emotions. The combination gives double sensual pleasure.

Texture – *smooth and rough*

Texture usually refers to the tactile sense, the feel; for example, velvet versus silk. In Jacobean appliqué texture refers to the visual sense. One color playing against another creates depth, thus giving the appearance of texture.

Tone – *grayness*

Tone refers to the grayness of a color which results from mixing complementary (opposite) colors. Examples of complementary colors illustrated on the color star are red and green, and red-purple and yellow-green. The resultant colors after mixing are toned down or muted. Observe nature. Look at the grass. In the sun the color of the grass looks bright, vibrant (high intensity); in the shade, somber, muted, grayed (toned down).

HARMONY

Just as there is harmony in music there is harmony in color. You know how you feel when a singer hits a sour note. You get the same sensation from color disharmony. Color combinations pulsate, either like a toothache (bad) or like a heartbeat (good). They can be energizing interactions or enervating conflicts. Those color combinations that tend to vibrate can usually be harmonized by toning down one color.

Analogous (neighboring) colors are always harmonious but often make a bland and uninteresting statement. A blue, blue-green, and green combination is pleasing, but lacks verve. Well-separated hues tend to produce discord. Near relatives cooperate; distant ones compete.

Too little harmony hurts our eyes; too much makes us yawn. Experimenting with your fabric stash will reveal which combinations are the most pleasing (harmonious) to you.

BALANCE – TRIANGLE RULE

Although called a rule, the Triangle Rule is really just a guide to check for color balance. If a specific color in a design falls on the three points of a triangle – any size, any type (right triangle, equilateral triangle, isosceles triangle), in any position – there is balance. There can be any number of triangles.

The Triangle Rule helps you avoid the monotony of color distribution and also helps keep a specific piece from leaping out and punching you in the nose. To check the color distribution in your quilt, choose one of the colors in your top and stick map pins into all the pieces of that color. See where it is distributed. Try this with other colors, with each block, and with the top as a whole. In checking for balance in your individual blocks and whole top, don't shackle yourself with this rule, but use it as a helper.

COLOR GLOSSARY

Analogous colors
neighbors on the color star, e.g., blue and green

Complementary colors
opposites on the color star, e.g., blue and orange

Hue
the name given to any color; used interchangeably with the word *color*

Intensity
brilliance of high or low degree

Primary color
pure color, does not involve any other color – red, blue, yellow

Scale
the size of the area of a color, e.g., in a print

Secondary color
a mixture of equal parts of any two primaries, e.g., purple from red and blue, green from blue and yellow, orange from yellow and red.

Shade
dark value of a color, e.g., burgundy (red with black), popularly used to refer to all the values of a color.

Temperature
warmth or coolness of a color

Texture
visual impression of depth, giving a three-dimensional effect

Tint
light value of a color, e.g., pink (white with red), often referred to as pastel

Tone
grayed values of a color, usually the result of mixing complements, e.g., red and green or blue-purple and yellow-orange

Value
lightness or darkness of a color

FABRIC

How does this discussion relate to fabric? An appreciation of the basic color concepts gives you confidence in your fabric choices.

BACKGROUND FABRIC

Choose your background fabric first. Traditional quiltmakers are inclined to think *muslin* because it has been so widely used for such a long time. Our forebears had little choice; their heirs have many choices. Neutral colors, either solid or visually textured, such as off-white, beige, eggshell, chamois, tan, and gray, permit a wide array of design fabrics and colors to be used for the appliquéd designs. A tone-on-tone print is pretty and gives depth, but if it's a resist print, it's often difficult to appliqué and to quilt. Black, also a neutral, works wonders, especially if it's a rich velvety black.

Other background colors are limiting. Non-neutrals such as wine, navy, purple, pink, brown, and green are a challenge. Yellow, orange, and turquoise are especially hard to use because they drastically limit design fabric choices.

When you're shopping for fabric, examine the weave. It should be straight and even. Ask that it be cut, not torn. Tearing bruises, stretches, and weakens the threads, requiring that part to be cut off. This means you have to allow for the waste. Resist bargain fabric, a poor place to economize. A 20-hour investment on an appliquéd block deserves high quality, evenly woven, cotton material.

DESIGN FABRIC

Although traditional Jacobean colors are soft and muted – greens, indigo blues, browns, roses, and golds – you don't need to be locked into that tradition. Tree trunks, leaves, stems, and vines can be done realistically in greens and browns, but flowers, in exhilarating reds, blues, pinks, purples, and yellows can be pure fantasy. Strange as it may seem, even though the patterns are based on antique designs, a Jacobean quilt can have a very contemporary look. You have the luxury of being able to use a broad palette of colors and a wide array of fabrics. Don't be afraid to use fabric scraps for your flowers: old prints, new hand-dyes, or even fashion fabrics.

Variety is the spice of life in Jacobean designs. How do you get variety? If you, like most quiltmakers, adore fabric and hoard it, now is the time to go through your treasure chest and choose those fabrics you'd like to use for your design pieces. Cruise the quilt shops and fabric stores. Buy fat quarters. Share with friends. Trade at your bee or guild. Invite a group to make a wallhanging with you and pool fabrics. Even if you all use the same fabrics, each finished quilt will be different, for it will have the maker's personal stamp on it. While you're gathering, pay no attention to "what goes with what" because you don't know, yet, in what combination you'll use them. A fabric can change from the way it looks solo to the way it appears in a duet or chorus. Not enough variety is sleep inducing; however, too much is nightmarish.

Be cautious about using solid colored fabrics. They tend to give a flat look, whereas prints, with their textured appearance, give depth. Use solids in no more than five percent of a block. Let the patterned fabrics predominate. If you really adore solids, go all the way with no prints at all. Prints of two colors or two shades of one color give visual texture, and a sense of depth never achieved by solids. For example, a black and brown combination print can look like the bark of a tree.

Pastels in Jacobean appliqué are not desirable, but if you can't live without them, team them up with prints of medium value for contrast. Avoid a lot of white in a print; it makes the piece itself look washed out or the white fades away if the background fabric is light and jumps out if the background fabric is dark.

Choose some small prints and some large prints. Large multicolored tropical prints offer variety and a look of hand-dyed fabric. A small leaf can be cut from a large print leaf, incorporating the printed veins. Thus, you can have a three-dimensional effect without the use of embroidery. If you use see-through templates, they can be placed over the exact section of the fabric design you want. Don't be afraid to make Swiss cheese out of a piece of fabric to get those parts you like.

Multicolored prints are busy and distracting. They cry out, "blend," but in Jacobean appliqué, don't feel locked into blending colors. You're not buying a wardrobe or decorating a room. Were you to introduce such a print, the viewer's eye would be drawn to it and it only. You want people to see the composition as a whole.

Marbled fabric and batiks can be overwhelming. Use them sparingly. Hand-dyed creations tantalize. Choose action-filled pieces with gradations from light to dark (several values). Light and dark contrast can create the illusion of illumination. Some hand-dyed fabrics are painted or have glitter added. If a piece feels stiff, it may be due to extra resin or salt in the painting process. If so, rinse the fabric in warm water. Of course, you can do your own dyeing, but don't underestimate the time and mess involved. Geometrics are rarely useful, but plaids and stripes are exciting. Include them.

To maintain color balance, you'll want to repeat some fabrics throughout the quilt. Still others, you'll sprinkle here and there for accent. High-octane colors like lipstick red, chartreuse, watermelon pink, mustard yellow, pumpkin orange, electric blue, and dazzling purple bring your quilt to life. "Fire" or "lightning" in fabric calls out, "look at me." Neighboring (analogous) colors are harmonious and go well together, but be cautious so that you don't overuse them and beget a blended top. Opposite (complementary) colors dazzle the eye when they are put side by side, so use them. Try any color and any combination of colors, but remember too much passion is fatiguing. Experiment; you can always replace a piece you don't like. When contrasts occur, the result is variety, stimulation, depth, movement, drama.

Don't stifle the impulse to try a combination. Go with the irresistible urge to experiment. Maintain your robust imagination in the use of fabric. Remember Jacobean appliqué is pure fantasy. Never forget color is personal. Be adventuresome! Keep in mind, however, that you want an exciting experience, not a wild party.

Fabric that is 100% cotton is the easiest of all fabric types to needle turn. The seam allowance rolls under with practically no effort. However, try other fabrics if you like. You can find good colors in blends, but they are less easy to work with than cottons. Rayon comes in beautiful patterns and shades, but it is contrary, rebellious, and hard to handle. It ravels badly and is very difficult to needle turn. Silks are lovely, but they tend to wrinkle and flatten after being stitched, and sometimes the stitches show. Wool is bulky, linen stiff, velvet heavy. But try any fabric that interests you.

Sometimes it's hard to tell 100% cotton from a blend. When shopping, look at the label on the end of the bolt. When using pieces from your treasure stash or that of a friend, burn a small piece in a fireproof container. If the ashes are of the *blow away* kind, it's 100% cotton; if a lump results, a synthetic is present.

Most of us have some color sense, and the rest of us can cultivate it. When you finish your Jacobean quilt, you'll be well on your cultivated way. With experimenting and hands-on experience, you'll grow braver and your color choices will be bolder. Your color awareness will also increase as you observe and analyze other people's work.

Appliqué permits more freedom in use of color than you have experienced in piecing, but if you are timid about color combinations, use this book's photos as a guide.

OTHER FABRICS

We recommend using the same fabric as the background for binding so that there is no competition with the designs. However, you might like to choose one of the dominant colors in the top and use that as a contrasting binding. The only other fabrics needed are for the backing and the sleeve.

Section 4

DESIGNING, MARKING & CUTTING

DESIGNING

Just thinking about colors and fabrics sets most quiltmakers to daydreaming about their next creation. Try sketching some of your ideas. Drawing your envisioned art work crystallizes those ideas and lets you see graphically potential variations.

The possibilities are many. The assists in this book include

• A large number of designs – 21

• Each design fits a 15" (38 cm) finished block or 16" (40.5 cm) cut block, so any design can be used in combination with any other single design or group of designs.

• Each design is approximately the same size so that the parts are interchangeable, proportionately speaking;

• An element of one design can be interchanged with an element of another design for a different look;

• A combination of elements from several designs can be used.

- Any design can be enlarged as a medallion;

- Mirrored images can be made, e.g., 2 blocks deep by 4 or 5 wide with the lower row in muted colors to look like a reflection;

- Some patterns for border designs are provided in this book on pp. 135–142. Create your own: repeat a favorite element from a block design, use a series of flower elements from different designs, join them with undulating vines, and scatter leaves for balance.

The one disadvantage of adapting the block designs to a border is that they are all intended to be placed vertically and may be a little awkward to adjust for the horizontal border pieces. Even so, you can use your imagination to create a fantasy border by turning the segments or by drawing some original flowers and leaves.

Start with the design miniatures in the right margin at the beginning of every section. These are printed for you to duplicate, to cut apart, to arrange in any pleasing combination. You can spend hours experimenting with the almost infinite possibilities. As you *play*, ask yourself: Where do I want my Jacobean quilt to hang? What finished size? Square or rectangular? Enlarged designs? Bordered? Predominant color? How many designs? Which ones? How set?

Follow your sketch with a cutting layout diagram that lets you figure the background fabric yardage. You don't have to be a math major to do the simple arithmetic because all the designs are set on the same size blocks (15" or 38 cm finished) unless you change the dimensions. If you do, your cutting size should be ½" (1.3 cm) larger on each side, whether block or border. Be sure to first lay out the border pieces, if a border is part of your plan, so that they can be cut without piecing. Then cut the blocks. The leftover fabric can be used for binding. Your drawing will show you how much background fabric yardage of 45" (114 cm) width fabric you will need. Be sure to choose a fine quality of 100% cotton that is evenly woven.

MASTER PATTERNS

You have the option of several materials for the master pattern: 1. interfacing (non-woven, non-fusible); 2. physician's examining table paper; or 3. freezer paper. Interfacing

Romantica #10, p. 84

Romantica #11, p. 88

Romantica #12, p. 92

is inexpensive, portable, and handles like fabric. Physician's paper and freezer paper are translucent, pliable, and strong.

1. Cut as many squares the size of your finished blocks as are needed.

2. On one square, trace with a fine felt tip permanent black pen the quadrants of the pattern you have chosen. Include on your master pattern the broken lines and the numbers identifying the templates. Your master pattern should look like the down-sized version, but the full-size you want. In one corner of the block write its identifying design number. Continue with other blocks.

3. If you include a border, figure out the length and width of the border pieces, which, in turn, depend on the size of the wall quilt. Cut out rectangles the finished size.

NEED TO KNOW

Q. Doesn't photocopying distort a pattern?

A. Yes, but minimally. It doesn't matter. There is freedom in appliqué not found in piecing.

TEMPLATES

Tulip template patterns for Design #5, #14, and border are provided on pp. 135–136. You'll make the other templates from your master patterns.

With a fine line permanent pen (if you want your lines to be permanent) or a lead pencil (if you want to wash off marks and have a clean template), trace the templates on clear plastic. Transparent plastic is ideal for letting you use the fabric to the best advantage because you can see the fabric underneath and choose the best area to cut the piece from. A permanent black line around the edge lets you see where the

template ends when it's placed on the fabric, but some people find this a distraction. A clean template ensures no accident of smudges on the fabric.

Identify each template with its piece number (Fig. 9). These numbers are for identification *only* and do *not* refer to the order of stitching. Pieces in a design that are the same shape have the same number, which means you need to make only one template for that piece, but as many design fabric pieces as are needed. "R" on the pattern means to turn the template over before marking that fabric piece.

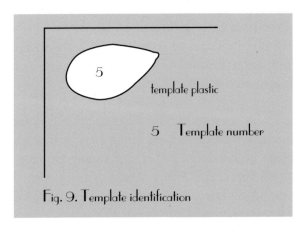

Fig. 9. Template identification

Cut out the templates of the design you have chosen. Store them in a plastic bag identified with the design number. Pin the bag to the master pattern for that block. Cut out the templates for the rest of the blocks, storing each group in an identified plastic bag and pinning each bag to the appropriate master pattern. Be sure to include the tulip templates on page 136 if you use Design #5 (page 64) or Design #14 (page 100).

You want to stitch perfect circles. A perfect circle template is the first step. You can use a professional circle template pattern purchased at an office supply store or you can trace the circles from the book pattern. When you cut out a circle template, make sure it's perfectly round. If it isn't, smooth the little jags with an emery board.

The illustrations in this book use solid lines to indicate stitching lines and broken lines to indicate cutting lines. This is the opposite of sewing patterns.

BACKGROUND FABRIC

To wash or not to wash is your call. Washing fabric before cutting is traditional, and you don't have to worry about the colors running or the fabric shrinking should you decide to wash the completed quilt. However, a wall quilt is not likely to become heavily soiled. Leaving fabrics unwashed preserves their brightness and maintains their crisp appearance. If you don't pre-wash, you can spend your washing time stitching.

Press the background fabric before cutting it. Cut your blocks 16" x 16" (40.5 x 40.5 cm) to finish 15" x 15" (38 x 38 cm), if you choose to make your blocks the same size as in the book. If you change the finished size, be sure to add ½" (1.3 cm) to your measurement on each of the four sides. Do the same with the border, but at each end, add the border width measurement. Be sure your width is in proportion to the top.

A straight evenly woven fabric ravels. You can pink all the raw edges. Zigzagging and serging can distort the piece. To ensure that all pieces are on grain and exactly the same size, use a T-square or a ruler and the lines on your cutting pad.

All the blocks need to be cut from the yardage in the same direction. Mixing crosscut pieces with lengthwise-cut pieces and/or reversing pieces can cause a difference in appearance. The background should look the same all over the quilt top. To avoid rotating or reversing the blocks, tag each as you cut it by stitching a small square of paper in the upper right-hand corner. Indicate *up* with an arrow.

MARKING

Find the center of the block by folding the square in half, then in half in the other direction. Make a light pencil mark on the *wrong* side where the fold lines intersect. Do the same for border pieces, if you are using a border.

To trace or not to trace the pattern on the background is a decision you need to make at this point. If you're timid or new to Jacobean appliqué and wish to have guiding lines on your background, follow Option A. Otherwise, try Option B on page 24.

OPTION A – MARKING BACKGROUND

Tape the master pattern to a flat surface. Line up the center of the background block and the center of the master pattern, then square the two. You can easily see through light colored fabric. Use a light box (discussed on p. 10) if you have a dark background.

We've been programmed for exact markings in needlework. If you mark exactly on the master pattern lines, you'll have to stitch exactly on those lines, which can at times be frustrating. Marks must be covered when doing appliqué, which is not always easy, so make as few, as light and inconspicuous as possible. A single line can serve for a tree trunk, stem, vine, or swirl. Mark other lines on the background fabric ⅛" to ¼" (.3 to .6 cm) inside the master pattern line to suggest where the pieces go. Put an *X* for placement of the small pieces. Judges notice pencil marks and sometimes walk right by a fantastic quilt because of them.

NEED TO KNOW

Q. Can I use a printed background fabric?

A. Great, but be cautious about resist prints; they are difficult to needle. Don't let background fabric compete with design fabrics.

Q. Isn't it hard to stitch on a black background?

A. No, because you're stitching on the design fabric, rather than the background fabric.

OPTION B – NOT MARKING BACKGROUND

An alternative to marking the design on the background fabric is to use the master pattern itself. When you're ready to stitch, baste the master pattern onto the background block across the top *only*, after first matching the centers and squaring the two. Place a design piece under the master pattern on the block in its appropriate place. Pin if needed, but pin on the back so that the thread doesn't catch on it. Lift the master pattern, flipping it over the top. Stitch that one piece in place. Neither hoop nor frame is used.

Appliquérs don't need to be captive to the color-within-the-lines mentality. If a piece is slightly off and there is a minimum of background markings, you won't have pencil marks to remove later. The no-marking method gives you freedom from total concentration and the frustration of trying to achieve perfect placement. Instead, you can daydream or watch the soaps.

MARKING DESIGN FABRIC

Separate your design fabric by color, type of print, etc. If two colors are dominant in one fabric, divide the piece in half and put a piece in each pile. Get well acquainted with your fabrics. Plan your block: tree trunk first, then flowers, and leaves last.

Lay the fabric right side up on your sandpaper board to keep it from shifting while you mark. Hold your pencil at an angle with the top tipped away from the template so that the pencil point angles into the template. This lets you mark close to the template and keep the point sharp. These marks will disappear when you needle turn, an appliqué technique explained later. Before marking be sure to flip the templates with numbers followed by "R".

There is an ongoing argument among appliqué teachers regarding cutting pieces on the straight or bias. Some judges insist that every appliquéd piece must be on the grain of the background fabric. Putting the design piece on its own straight is handicap enough, but having to put it on the straight of the background fabric is a double handicap.

Bias is 100 times easier to needle turn than a piece on grain and there is minimal fraying and raveling. Compare the areas of most and least raveling on each of the ovals in Fig. 10 or demonstrate to yourself whether you want your pieces on the straight or the bias. Cut two small ovals, one on the straight and one on the bias. Appliqué each on a scrap of fabric. Which ravels more? Your oval on the straight or your oval on the bias?

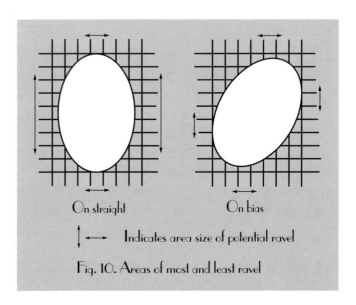

On straight   On bias

↕ ←→ Indicates area size of potential ravel

Fig. 10. Areas of most and least ravel

Grain going a number of different ways in your design pieces lends interest. Artists who paint short lines crossing one another haphazardly in every direction achieve texture. Similarly, the appliquér produces texture by using the bias of the fabric. Cut as many pieces as possible on the bias. Don't hesitate to use a printed leaf for your leaf piece, cutting a small leaf to appliqué from a large printed one. So that the printed veins become the veins of your leaf, use a see-through template. Choose areas in a tropical print just the right shade for a lovely flower regardless of grain.

CUTTING

Cut the pieces out with an added ⅛" (.3 cm) turn-under allowance. Yes, ⅛", not ¼" (.6 cm). Less is better than more because the more allowance you have, the more you have to tuck under. A wide turn-under allowance creates a lump like dirt under a rug.

When cutting points, keep the tips pointed as in Fig. 11. There's no need to blunt cut the end.

NEED TO KNOW

Q. Do I cut out the pieces for the whole block before I start to stitch?

A. Yes. You want to look at the block composition as a whole, checking on harmony and balance.

On the inside of the tulip there are a straight edge and a scalloped edge. You'll notice that the space between these two edges allows for only one turn-under allowance, not two. Cut the fabric so that the allowance is on the scalloped side as in Fig. 12. When you stitch, you will overlap the two petals of the tulip, hiding the raw edge. Cut a small rectangle of contrasting fabric to place inside the *cup* of the tulip before overlapping the petals. For specific instructions and templates see pp. 134–136.

After cutting a design fabric piece, pin it in place on the background fabric block. Following the composition check of your blocks (page 26), remove the pieces from the background fabric and pin them in place on your master pattern. This then becomes your portable *storage* block. If you plan not to mark on the background fabric, the master pattern will be basted to the top of your background fabric block, as explained on page 24, so you will need to cut another square of interfacing or scrap muslin for your *storage* block. Pin the pieces on it in their approximate positions.

BIAS PIECES

Measure the amount of bias strips needed for the stems in the designs you have chosen; e.g., Design #12 on pages 92–95 requires 17" (43 cm). Choose the fabrics you would like to use for these. Every stem can be different, all the stems in one design can be the same, or all the stems in the entire quilt can be the same. Be sure to press the material before cutting. Rotary cut a minimum of 1" (2.5 cm) widths.

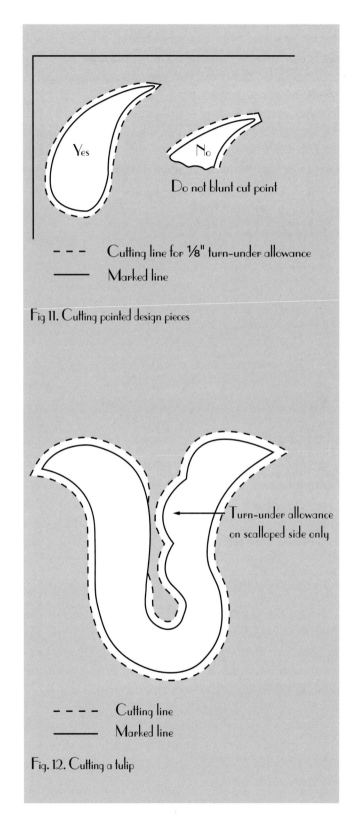

- - - - Cutting line for ⅛" turn-under allowance
——— Marked line

Fig 11. Cutting pointed design pieces

- - - - Cutting line
——— Marked line

Fig. 12. Cutting a tulip

You want perfect bias pieces to make the stems, not only to be pretty, but to lie flat. If all the stems are to be made from the same fabric, you might use the continuous bias method, explained in many sewing books. However, you *must* cut absolutely accurately to get a perfect bias. Many people can't cut without getting slightly off; "slightly off" is bad news for appliquéd stems. If the cut is not accurately on the bias, it will ripple, whereas true bias curves well. Cut away any bias seams that show because they are not pretty.

NEED TO KNOW

Q. Is the tree trunk always only one fabric?

A. It can be one or several. Try the leaf shading technique explained on page 34.

Q. What about the fabric in the center of the tulip?

A. It's a rectangle tucked underneath. See page 25.

A square with individual pieces cut on the bias is more accurate than cutting continuous bias. A 9" (22.5 cm) square will yield 72" (182.5 cm) of 1" (2.5 cm) strips. After marking the right side, lay the strips aside to be used later.

BINDING STRIPS

If you like a contrast binding, pick out one of the dominant colors in your top and use that fabric for the binding. It makes an attractive frame. If you prefer to use a border, let it act as the frame, with the binding the same as the background fabric.

Cut the strips on the straight. Then cut the ends of the strips at a perfect 45 degree angle so they are ready for sewing. After tagging the right sides, lay the strips aside for later.

You can make a double binding if you prefer the look of a thicker edge. With a wall quilt you don't need to be concerned about wear, which is usually the reason for a double binding.

You can use binding cut on the bias instead of straight strips. A bias binding must be sewn on the quilt with great care to avoid stretching and a wavy edge. Finger press the bias seams, rather than ironing them, for the same reason.

COMPOSITION

Here's where the Styrofoam board plays a part. As you cut each design piece, pin it in its approximate position on a background fabric square. When all the pieces are placed, pin the block to the styrofoam board. Step back and look at your block in terms of color, contrast, harmony, and balance. Squint your eyes. Look through a reducing glass or the reverse end of binoculars. Take a Polaroid picture. Let the block sit overnight and look at it again in the morning.

Two other tricks for checking color and balance:

1. Turn the block upside down and walk several feet away to view it. If the color and balance are correct, the block will be pleasing. If something is wrong, it will look as if the flower is falling out of the picture.

2. Hold a mirror in front of the block and look at its reflection. Because you are looking at the composition instead of the flower itself, a problem area will pop out.

You can also check for color balance by using the Triangle Rule explained on page 17. You want your top to sparkle, but not to startle. Don't let the eye become fixed on one spot; it should cruise the entire top. Place the blocks in the area where you plan to hang your quilt when it's finished because lighting is very important and affects the appearance of the colors. Does any part jump at you? Do you see a *hole*? Don't be afraid to reject a piece and cut a new one. Anything you don't like, change, even a tree trunk that may not fit with the flowers and leaves you have added. Stitching will neither improve the color nor make you like it better.

When deciding which design fabric you want to use, especially if you are replacing a flower piece, bundle up one of the fabrics in a circle between your thumb and forefinger, making it look like a flower. Fold other fabrics around it. Choose those that make the combination look vibrant.

You can choose to cut the design pieces for the entire top or to cut pieces for several blocks and look at them together. Then cut several more. Repeat some fabrics; bring in some new ones. Watch for very bright blocks versus very dull blocks. Check on contrast and color balance of each group and then again for the whole top. When you're happy with the placement of your design pieces, transfer them to your portable square.

If a group is making Jacobean appliqué quilts, members can examine one another's blocks, point out what they like, and make suggestions for those areas that bother them. That's what the participants in one of our workshops did; they fastened their blocks on the wall for critique and these are some of the comments.

"When I saw you were going to use that saffron colored background fabric, I thought you're gonna get into trouble, but you pulled it off."

"Those greens are like real!"

"Maybe Block #3 ought to be traded with Block #17. You've got two same-color-looks together."

"Block #6 is Dullsville; needs to be punched up."

"Look what that bright orange did. Wow!"

"The pale blue background fabric looks pretty."

"The printed veins on that leaf look embroidered."

"Where'd you get the gold? I need a piece of that."

"How many different fabrics have you got in that top?"

"Do you ever have an eye for color!"

You'll learn about color from one another. Expect to get braver and expect the colors to get brighter as you make more and more blocks. Improvise. Don't hesitate to replace a flower with a bird, add a butterfly, or put a small animal at the base of the tree in the spirit of antique Jacobean designs. Give the quilt your stamp of individuality.

Tulip from Design #5 showing the difference in visual interest created by using related or contrasting colors (see p. 15).

$\mathscr{S}$ection 5

STITCHING FUN

Have the following items ready before you start stitching: needles, pins, scissors, thimble, master pattern, background fabric block, design fabric pieces on your portable squares, and matching threads. Remember to match the thread to the design fabric, not the background fabric, and if you don't have the exact shade, go one shade darker, never lighter.

Create a stitching *nest* for pleasant hours of stitching. Seat yourself in a chair that fits. Put your feet up. This makes you lean back, not forward, a more relaxed position. Hold the stitching piece loosely in your lap, on a pillow, or with a lapboard under it. To maintain a comfortable position that will allow many hours of stitching time, the thumb of the hand holding the background fabric must face the thumb of the stitching hand (Fig.13). Don't twist your holding hand; that will hunch up your shoulder, causing fatigue. Try a pillow under your holding arm. Periodically shake the tension out of your hands as if shaking off water. If you break for five minutes every hour, for an hour at lunch and an hour at dinner, you can stitch from early in the morning until late at night.

STARTING

The order in which you stitch the pieces does not matter except where pieces overlap. Overlaps are shown by arrows. The shaft of the arrow is the *under* piece;

the arrow point, the *over* piece (Fig. 14). Some stitchers like to mark arrows on all their master patterns. See a sample for Design #10 on pages 84–87. The arrows act as reminders and let you move around the block, which is much more entertaining than stitching one area at a time. You might do all the *under* pieces for that design first, so you won't forget later. The part of a piece that is under another piece doesn't have to be stitched down. Generally move only one piece at a time from your storage block to your background fabric square, except for the flowers. Move the whole flower unit and pin it in place, remembering to put the pins on the back.

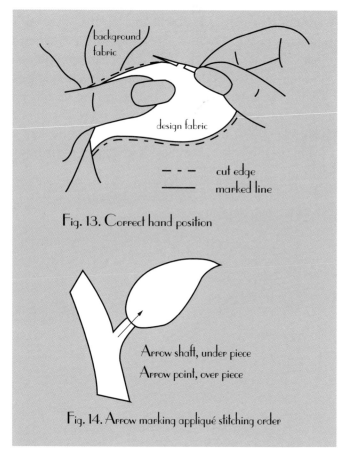

Fig. 13. Correct hand position

Arrow shaft, under piece
Arrow point, over piece

Fig. 14. Arrow marking appliqué stitching order

A dark fabric will show through a pale one, which is unattractive. When that occurs, cut a piece of inexpensive voile, organza, or organdy the same size as your template, without adding a turn-under allowance. Sandwich it between the dark and the light pieces. It acts like a slip under a dress or skirt.

Cut a thread (matching the design fabric piece, not the background fabric), 15" to 18" (38 cm to 46 cm) long. A longer piece will tangle or fray. Cut the thread on an angle; thread the needle and knot the thread all on the same end,

Romantica #13, p. 96

Romantica #14, p. 100

Romantica #15, p. 104

the one that comes off the spool last. Use any knot you like: the one your mama taught you, the so-called quilter's knot, or your own creation. A workshop participant claims that running the needle and thread through a fabric softener dryer sheet keeps the thread from twisting.

NEED TO KNOW

Q. Should I baste?

A. As little as possible. Only very large pieces such as the tree trunks may need to be thread basted to keep them from shifting. If basting makes you less anxious, pin, putting the pins on the back.

The easiest place to start stitching is on a *straight-away* or on a gentle curve. Usually the tree trunk is a good starting place. You don't want to start at a point. After completing one design, you will have a *feel* for the stitching order. Because tree trunks are usually the largest piece in the design, you may want to thread baste them.

Anchor your knot under the seam allowance of the design fabric so the knot will be hidden in the fold. Stitch counterclockwise (lefties, clockwise). This means the turn-under allowance is away from you, not toward you. Your thumb holding the piece is directly below your stitching (Fig. 15).

NEEDLE TURNING

With the tip of your needle about ¾" (2 cm) from where the thread comes up in the fold, sweep the needle toward you, turning the seam allowance under. Take several stitches and repeat. Always turn with your needle, never with your fingers. This technique eliminates pressing or basting. If the edge is not smooth, perhaps you are not sweeping under enough. A big sweep, ¾"– 1" (2 – 2.5 cm), keeps the edge smooth; a little sweep makes peaks.

Directly out from where the needle emerges on the marked line and slightly under the fold of the design fabric, insert your needle point into the background fabric, pick up two or three threads and come up into the design fabric on the marked line (the fold) about ¹⁄₁₆" (.15 cm) from the last stitch. The picking up of the threads and the emergence into the fold are one motion (Fig. 16). Don't fret if the stitches on the back go in different directions; focus on having elegant stitches that don't show on the front.

Make your stitches perpendicular to the edge of the design piece. This will line up the stitches. The arrows in Fig. 17 show the angles of the stitches, not the distance from the fold. Jacobean appliqué technique emphasizes the design and hides the stitching. If you take a stitch too far out from the design piece into the background fabric, it will show. If you take it too deep into the design fabric, it will show and also dimple the fabric. Stitches that are too tight fray the

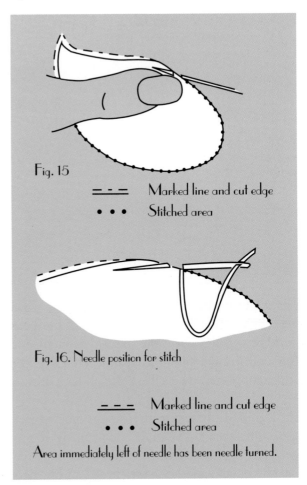

Fig. 15

— — — Marked line and cut edge

• • • Stitched area

Fig. 16. Needle position for stitch

— — — Marked line and cut edge

• • • Stitched area

Area immediately left of needle has been needle turned.

thread and ripple the design piece. If the stitches are not close enough, some of the threads from the design fabric piece may peek out. Take your needle and push the threads back in. There is no such thing as fray or ravel when you're stitching; consider it part of your turn-under allowance and tuck it under with your needle. There also is no such thing as ripping. It's *unstitching*, as a child told her mother. Try not to *unstitch* because some threads stay in the background fabric – little fussy things that judges don't like.

NEED TO KNOW

Q. Which piece do I appliqué first?

A. Start with the tree trunk, which is usually your biggest piece. Before you start stitching, make sure which pieces will be overlapped. Do the "under" pieces first.

Continue; needle turn the allowance, insert your needle barely under the design fabric into the background fabric, pick up two or three threads, come up into the fold from underneath, needle turn, pick up two or three threads, come up into the fold, needle turn. A rhythm and a constant tension on the thread, like in crochet or knitting, will produce stitches that are consistent and beautiful. To avoid discomfort in your wrists and shoulders, be sure your thumbs keep facing each other.

Follow the steps, imitating this method, for a few days. If you don't like it, go back to your old method or someone else's method. Do it the way you like, the way you can get the best precision stitching.

To summarize the secret to hiding Jacobean appliqué stitches:

• Thread that matches the design fabric piece exactly

• Coming up into the design fabric piece in the fold

• Going down into the background fabric a fraction under the fold and directly out in a straight line

• Pulling the stitch snug, but not so snug that it dimples the fabric.

STOPPING

When your thread is too short to continue, push the needle through to the back of the background fabric, in from the edge of the design piece. Take a little *bite* of the fabric with the needle. Make a loop of the thread and hold it under your thumb as you gently pull the stitch in place (Fig. 18, Step 1). Repeat with a second *bite* (Fig. 18, Step 2). Bury the tail by passing the needle between the two layers (background fabric and design fabric) away from the edge. Snip the tail close to the background fabric so there are no loose threads.

To continue stitching, cut a new piece of thread and knot it. Start with the needle point coming up at the marked line, very close to the last stitch. The new knot will be hidden in the fold. Proceed as before.

After the piece is appliquéd, end as you did when you ran out of thread. You don't want any loose threads showing through the background fabric.

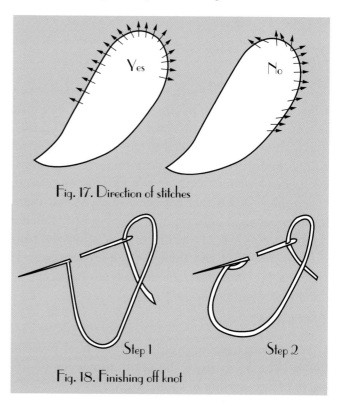

Fig. 17. Direction of stitches

Fig. 18. Finishing off knot

NEED TO KNOW

Q. Must I stitch through all the fabric layers?

A. It's not necessary. Just be sure that at least two layers of fabric are connected.

Q. What if a dark design piece placed under a light design piece shows through?

A. Let it wear a slip as you would under a sheer dress. Cut a piece of voile, organza, or organdy the same shape as your template (do not add turn-under allowance) and sandwich it between the dark and the light pieces.

CURVES

CONVEX

Convex curves, outside curves, are easy (Fig. 19). Choose a piece to appliqué that has a gentle convex curve. You don't need to clip the curve because the turn-under allowance is only ⅛" (.3 cm) rather than ¼" (.6 cm).

CONCAVE

Concave curves, inside curves, are a little harder. Clip when absolutely necessary, which will be rarely because of the narrow seam allowance (Fig. 20). You'll know when you need to clip because you'll feel a drag on the needle or the seam fold won't stay fold-ed. Listen to your fabric. It will talk to you, saying, "Clip me." When this happens, obey. When there are two curves, a concave and a convex one, called a double curve (Fig. 21), as in a branch, stitch the con-cave (inside) first and then the convex (outside). If the outside is done first, the inside tends to pucker.

U-TURNS

You should have no problem with a *U*, if you clip every ⅛" (.3 cm) into the seam allowance of the curve before starting to stitch (Fig. 22).

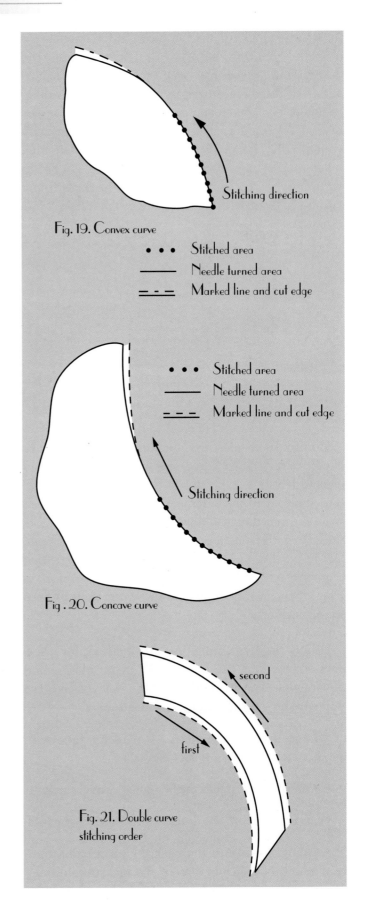

Fig. 19. Convex curve

• • • Stitched area
——— Needle turned area
– – – Marked line and cut edge

• • • Stitched area
——— Needle turned area
– – – Marked line and cut edge

Stitching direction

Fig. 20. Concave curve

second

first

Fig. 21. Double curve stitching order

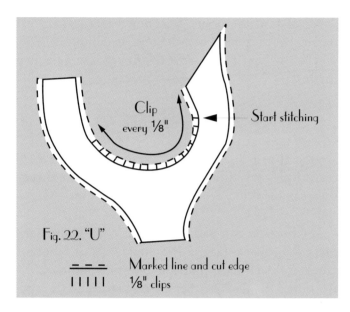

Fig. 22. "U"

- - - Marked line and cut edge
| | | | | ⅛" clips

POINTS

This method will give you beautiful points. The instructions may sound complicated, but if you follow them step by step, you'll be delighted with the results.

1. Stitch, not to the end of the fabric, but to the marked point, the point where you start down the other side (Fig. 23, Step 1).

2. Take a second stitch on top of the last stitch (in the exact same spot) to secure that stitch, thus keeping it from loosening.

3. Take your thimble off and set your threaded needle in the background fabric, out of the way.

4. Turn your block as if you were going to start stitching down the other side.

5. Clip off any little tail from the first side seam allowance that noses out (Fig. 23, Step 2).

6. Hold the thread and the stitch at the point with the tip of your thumbnail.

7. With a quilter's pin grasped about ½" (1.3 cm) up from the point and braced from behind with your middle finger to strengthen it (shorter is stronger), sweep the turn-under allowance from right to left. Then sweep it back from left to right (left-handers sweep it left to right and then right to left). Holding the point with your thumbnail, release it only when you sweep the fabric under. If you don't like the result, pull the turn-under allowance out with your needle, and try again. To repeat: sweep the needle away from you, then sweep it toward you, carefully tucking under the allowance.

Sometimes frays at the point cause panic for the stitcher. Don't let them intimidate you. Remember the remaining threads are in the allowance. Just sweep them under and stitch. If you let yourself get frustrated, the situation will worsen.

8. Still holding the point tightly, turn the block so you can take a stitch into the background fabric about ¹⁄₁₆" (.15 cm) out from the point (Fig. 23, Step 3). Unlike the other stitches which you've been try-

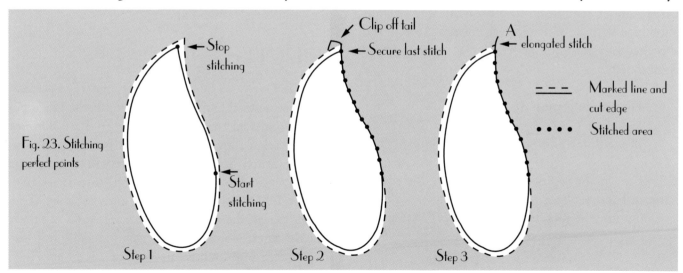

Fig. 23. Stitching perfect points

Step 1 — Stop stitching / Start stitching

Step 2 — Clip off tail / Secure last stitch

Step 3 — A elongated stitch

- - - Marked line and cut edge
• • • • Stitched area

ing to hide, you now want this one to show. That extra stitch elongates the point. It will give the illusion that the tip is more pointed than it really is.

9. Proceed with stitching down the other side. When the appliquéd piece is finished, use your needle to shape the point and the heat of your thumb to press it.

After a week of using this point technique, you'll be making perfect points without even thinking about it. The quilter's pin is the tool, but the real secret is the ⅛" (.3 cm) turn-under allowance.

SKINNY LEAVES

Sometimes there are skinny leaves or ends of slender tendrils with sharp points. Even with these you can make perfect points.

1. Proceed as you did with points as explained earlier, stitching to the marked end of the leaf.

2. Take another stitch on top of the last stitch to secure it.

3. Turn the stem back on itself and trim away any extra turn-under allowance near the point on the side you've just stitched. Also clip away any loose threads that will be a hindrance or add bulk. This is fat removal, liposuction by scissors.

4. Hold your thumbnail on the last stitch with the thread under your thumb, out of the way of your stitching. With a quilt pin, sweep right to left and then left to right (lefties, sweep left to right and then right to left).

5. Make an elongating stitch at the point.

6. Turn and start down the other side.

7. If the point is still too wide, weave the thread back and forth across the point with your needle, catching only the turn-under allowance. Do not pull too tightly because you will distort the shape.

A bump at the point? Too much fabric is turned under. Beat it gently with scissors as tailors do. Now you know that *points with skinny tips are hard* is a myth.

LEAF SHADING

As a spin-off of Nancy Pearson's *twisted ribbon* technique, try this way to make a shaded three-dimensional leaf.

1. Choose a two-part leaf or cut a large leaf template lengthwise (Fig. 24, Step 1). Use a different fabric for each part, light for one side and dark for the other. Remember when cutting apart, add a turn-under allowance on the inside of each piece.

2. Clip the turn-under allowance to the marked line across from each other on both inside pieces of the leaf (Fig. 24, Step 2). Overlap dark and light parts alternately.

3. Using two needles and two shades of thread, stitch, making one section an *under*, and the other section an *over*. In Step 2, *1* is *under*, and *2* is *over*.

4. Stitch the outside edges.

Design #12 has a leaf in the lower right quadrant (p. 95) that shows two short lines across what would be the vein line. This shading technique will work easily on this leaf. Look for other pieces that lend themselves to leaf shading.

CIRCLES

Perfect circles result from being: 1. marked perfectly, 2. cut perfectly, and 3. stitched perfectly. Use a pin on the underside to hold the circle in place. Do not clip the seam allowance. Needle turn only enough to take one stitch. Turning under more will create points or a straight line. Take one stitch, turn the circle. Continue. Occasionally a circle ends looking like a spiral; that is, the last part of the circle does not meet exactly where you started. If this happens, snip the beginning knot, take out two or three stitches,

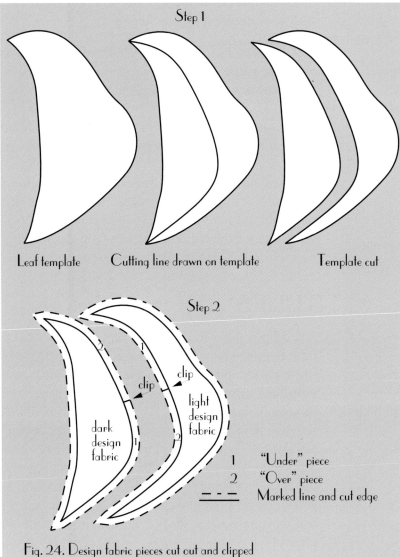

Step 1

Leaf template — Cutting line drawn on template — Template cut

Step 2

clip

clip

dark design fabric

light design fabric

1   "Under" piece
2   "Over" piece
– – –   Marked line and cut edge

Fig. 24. Design fabric pieces cut out and clipped

DEEP VALLEYS (heart flip)

1. Clip at the V to the marked line. If you clip too deeply into the fabric, don't worry. Just make the V a little deeper (Fig. 25, Step 1).

2. Stitch to the V (Fig. 25, Step 2).

3. Fold under the loose side (Fig. 25, Step 3).

4. Take a stitch the same size as the others, no bigger, no smaller.

5. Press with your thumb.

6. Slowly bring the folded part back up.

7. When you flip the folded part back, the turn-under allowance on the flipped part turns under, ready for you to continue stitching. If stitches at the V show, it's okay, as long as they are no bigger than Lilliputian chicken feet.

reshape the circle, and finish stitching. One circle may take 10 minutes to do, but it will be beautiful. Treat ovals like circles. To repeat: needle turn for only one stitch, take that one stitch, turn. People will rave over the symmetry of your circles.

VALLEYS

Some valleys are deep (like hearts) and some, shallow (like scallops). To make both types well-defined *V's* and not *U's*, two different techniques are used: *heart-flip* for the deep valleys and *working-backward* for the shallow ones.

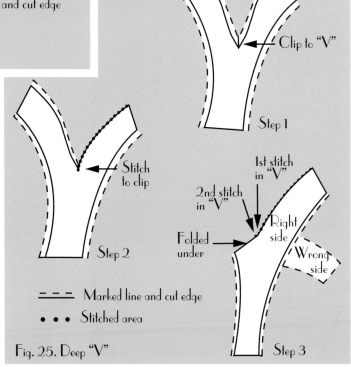

Clip to "V"

Step 1

Stitch to clip

Step 2

1st stitch in "V"

2nd stitch in "V"

Right side

Folded under

Wrong side

– – –   Marked line and cut edge
• • •   Stitched area

Fig. 25. Deep "V"

Step 3

SHALLOW VALLEYS (working backward)

1. Clip at the V (Fig. 26, Step 1).

2. Stitch to the V (Fig. 26, Step 2).

3. Start needle turning about 1½" to 2" (3.8 cm to 5 cm) away from the last stitch. Needle turn in tiny increments, working back down to the last stitch, shaping the curve. Take one anchor stitch after last stitch at V (Fig. 26, Step 3).

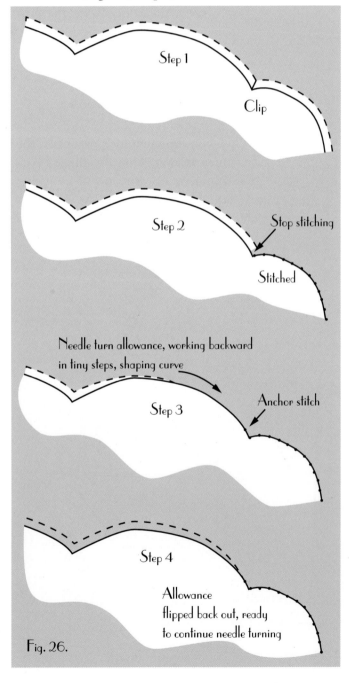

Step 1

Clip

Step 2

Stop stitching

Stitched

Needle turn allowance, working backward in tiny steps, shaping curve

Step 3

Anchor stitch

Step 4

Allowance flipped back out, ready to continue needle turning

Fig. 26.

4. Flip out the allowance that you've turned under with your needle (Fig. 26, Step 4).

5. Proceed from the V, needle turning enough for only one stitch. Take that stitch and needle turn for the next stitch. Repeat as in a circle.

6. Continue until you come to the next V, when you will repeat the above steps.

When stitching a tree trunk or branch, stitch one side and flip the rest down, using the heart-flip technique. If you have already stitched some part of the other side of the trunk or branch, use the working-backwards technique.

TULIPS

A tulip appears in Design #5 and Design #14. The tulip template patterns are shown on pages 135–136. Place the template on as much design fabric bias as possible. (Left-handers: flip the tulip template when placing it on the design fabric. The non-scalloped side will then be on the right, ready for you to stitch clockwise.) There is no hump at the fabric base of the tulip when you stitch, as you might expect, because the side is pivoted only slightly. A tulip piece will let you show off your skill in stitching a *U*, several *Vs*, and two perfect points. See specific instructions on page 134.

BUTTING UP

When two pieces touch each other without overlapping, it's called *butting up*. There is a natural tendency to start the second piece at the point of contact, but sometimes by the time that piece is completely stitched, the contact point either overlaps or falls short of meeting. If it overlaps, some can be cut off, but if it falls short of meeting, there is trouble and you have to unstitch. The following will help keep the two pieces aligned (Fig. 27).

1. Stitch the first piece (a) down completely.

2. Pin the second piece (b) in place.

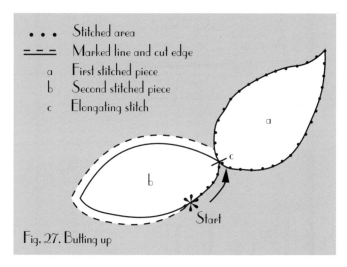

- • • • Stitched area
- - - - Marked line and cut edge
- a First stitched piece
- b Second stitched piece
- c Elongating stitch

Fig. 27. Butting up

3. Start about 1" (2.5 cm) from where you want them butted, stitching toward the point of contact.

4. Make an elongating stitch to ensure that the pieces touch.

5. Continue stitching around the piece to your starting point.

BIAS STEMS

You probably cut bias pieces for stems when you were marking and cutting other design fabric pieces. But if you are cutting them now, remember the pieces need to be on the true bias and no narrower than 1" (2.5 cm). There are a number of ways to appliqué bias pieces. Choose the way that feels right for you.

OPTION A – GRANDMOTHER'S WAY

Fold in thirds and baste. One raw edge is inside and the other is underneath when you stitch.

OPTION B – COMMERCIAL GADGETS

Follow the manufacturer's instructions.

OPTION C – CENTER BASTE

With the bias unfolded, pin the bias onto the background fabric where the stem is to be placed. In order to make sure the marked line is covered, make a running stitch a fraction to the left of the *middle* of the bias but on the *center* of the stem design.

Trim away the extra fabric of the bias to the right of and close to the running stitch. Fold the left side over and turn the raw edge under. Pin and stitch. This method is good if you want the bias narrow in one area and wide in another or if you have long stems or vines. Don't choose this method for deep curves, e.g., a grapevine tendril, because it won't curve nicely.

OPTION D – SEWING MACHINE ADAPTER

Fold the fabric right sides together. Use the guide to keep the sewing line perfect, after choosing the width desired. If you sew a lot of bias, you need one of these wonderful attachments.

Use the double curve technique (p. 32) when appliquéing bias. Stitch the inside curve first and then the outside curve. The piece will lie perfectly flat. With the reverse, you'll discover little gathers on the inside that you won't like. Roll leftover bias onto a cardboard cylinder and save for future projects.

NEED TO KNOW

Q. Do I match the thread to the design fabric or the background fabric?

A. Always match your design fabric.

Q. What size seam allowances shall I use?

A. Generally, for sewing (machine work), leave a ¼" (.6cm) seam allowance. For handwork (stitching), allowances are called turn-under allowances and are ⅛" (.3 cm) or ¹⁄₁₆" (.15 cm).

Section 6

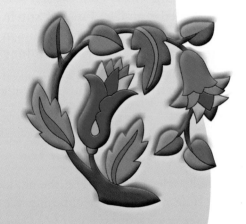

FINISHING UP

ASSEMBLING

In Section 4 (p. 23), we suggested that you mark the center of each background fabric block (and border pieces) before appliquéing.

1. Now measure an equal distance out from that marked center in all four directions 7½" (19 cm) if you're making the squares the same size as the book patterns. The designs were created to fit a 15" (38 cm) finished block. With a T-square or ruler, draw lines for sewing on the wrong side of all four sides. If your blocks are not all the same size, use the smallest one and measure the others by it. Remember you need at least ¼" (.6 cm) all around for seaming.

An option is to make a square of cardboard or plastic the size you want. Find the center by drawing diagonal lines. Where the lines intersect, punch a small hole with the point of a compass or scissors. Put a pin through the hole and into the pencil mark on the back of your block. Square the template with the block, and draw around the four sides with a pencil. These will be your sewing lines.

2. Pin your blocks together and sew along the marked lines.

3. Trim excess fabric, leaving ¼" (.6 cm) for the seam allowance.

4. Press to one side or open, as you prefer. Pressing seams open makes quilting easier.

OPTIONAL BORDER

1. Appliqué each strip, leaving unfinished at each end the number of inches that your border is wide plus 3"; for example, if the width of your finished border is 6" (15 cm), stop appliquéing 9" (23 cm) from each end. The corners will be completed after the border pieces are sewn to the top and mitered.

2. Mark the center of each strip and each side of the top. Pin strip and top together, matching centers.

3. Sew within ¼" (.6 cm) of the corner. Pin and sew the other border strips.

4. Fold border strip back onto top, right sides together. Pin.

5. Mark the miter angle from the point where the two border strips meet, using the 45 degree angle line on your cutting pad. Mark the adjoining strip in the same way. Pin the two strips together, matching marked lines. Sew from the inner corner to the outer corner.

6. Check for accuracy. Does it lie flat? If not, re-do. If it does, trim the seam to ¼" (.6 cm).

7. Repeat for the other corners.

8. Complete all unfinished appliqué.

9. Gently press the entire top on the wrong side with a *dry* iron.

BATTING AND BACKING

1. Cut the batting a little larger than the top.

2. Cut the backing a little larger than the batt. The backing is larger than the other layers so that you can fold the excess fabric to the front and baste it in place to protect the edge of the quilt during quilting.

3. Lay the backing right side down on a table or floor, then the batt, and then the top, right side up.

4. Pin baste or thread baste.

Romantica #16, p. 108

Romantica #17, p. 112

Romantica #18, p. 116

QUILTING

Quilting can be done in the open spaces and around the designs. One suggestion is to shadow quilt ⅛" (.3 cm) and echo quilt three rows ¼" (.6 cm) apart out from the design. Stippling or meandering quilting in the spaces where the blocks come together gives the whole top depth. Some of the flower and leaf templates can be used as quilting patterns. Hanging diamonds or crosshatch, especially doubles, also works. Use quilting thread the hue of your background fabric so that your quilting design doesn't compete with your appliquéd design.

When the quilting is completed, sew with a machine basting stitch ⅛" (.3 cm) in from the outside edge of the top all the way around. Trim the excess batting and backing even with the quilt top.

SLEEVE

Most quiltmakers know how to make a sleeve for hanging their quilt. If you do not know, check books in your collection for instructions. You can sew it on prior to the binding or afterwards, as you prefer. A second sleeve can be attached to the bottom so that the weight of an inserted dowel will help it hang well. You can, instead, sew washers, drapery squares, or fishing weights into the lower corners. Make sure they are well hidden.

BINDING

You have already cut strips for the binding. Sew them together. Gently finger press the seams. Ironing may cause stretching, which may, in turn, cause the binding to wave.

You can sew the binding (double or single, whichever you prefer) to the top using "true" miters, as just discussed, or with "false" miters.

"FALSE" MITERS

Sew the binding to the quilt top as follows:

1. Lay the binding, right side to right side, on the quilt top, keeping the edges even. Start sewing about 6" (15 cm) from a corner, leaving a 2" (5 cm) tail unsewn. Fig. 28, Step 1. Sew carefully, maintaining an even ¼" (.6 cm) seam.

2. Stop sewing ¼" (.6 cm) from the corner. Backstitch and clip the thread. Fig. 28, Step 2.

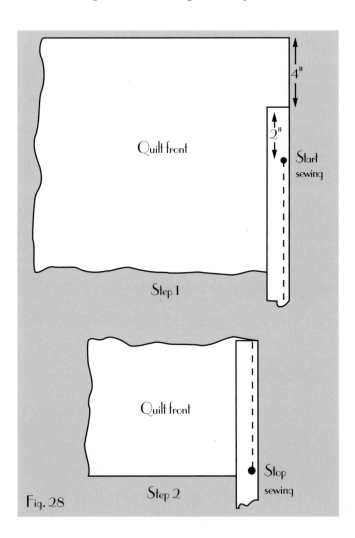

Fig. 28

3. Turn the quilt to the next edge.

4. Fold the binding on the diagonal (Fig. 28, Step 3) and then fold it back even with the top and side edges (Fig. 28, Step 4).

5. Starting at the upper edge, sew a ¼" (.6 cm) seam to within ¼" (.6 cm) of the next corner.

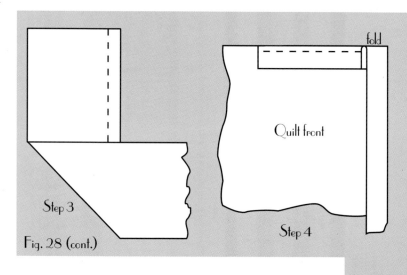

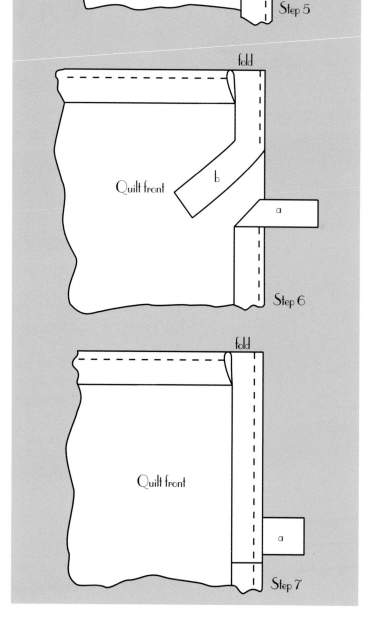

Step 3

Fig. 28 (cont.)

6. Repeat the previous steps at each corner.

7. About 2" (5 cm) from the end, stop sewing. Cut off the remaining binding, leaving a tail of 4" (10 cm) (Fig. 28, Step 5).

8. Fold the bottom piece (a) back diagonally (Fig. 28, Step 6).

9. Hold and sew the end piece (b) to meet the first sewing (Fig. 28, Step 7).

10. Trim the excess fabric.

11. Turn the binding to the wrong side, fold under ¼" (.6 cm), pin, and stitch, using your newly-learned hidden appliqué technique. The stitches can be ¼" (.6 cm) apart rather than the ¹⁄₁₆" (.15 cm) you used on the design pieces.

When you come to the corner, tack the miters down well, front and back. Be sure the corners are square. Push the needle back to the stitching line and continue stitching. At the point where the binding joins, trim excess, and stitch the front and back with your hidden stitch in such a way that it's hard to tell where you started and where you stopped. Don't press the binding; it tends to cause stretching. Quilt one row around the quilt on the inside of the binding.

Section 7

Competing & Celebrating

SIGNATURE

Future generations deserve to know about your Jacobean quilt.

1. Make a fabric label, indicating the quilt name, your name, the date, and any other information you think your progeny might like to know.

2. If you iron freezer paper on the back of your label before writing on it, you'll find you can write with ease, especially if you use a sandpaper board under it. Remove the paper backing before attaching the label to your quilt.

3. Use a fine point permanent ink pen to write on the fabric. Consider decorating the label with your logo or with Jacobean flowers. Some quiltmakers have success using the typewriter, word processor, or computer printer for the label information.

4. Heat set the label with a dry iron.

5. Stitch the label onto the back of your quilt.

6. Take a photograph of your quilt for your scrapbook (and for insurance purposes).

You have created a family heirloom. Show it with pride.

COMPETITION PRIMER

HOW TO BECOME FAMOUS

Pick up any quilt magazine and you'll see an announcement of a contest of some type somewhere some time. A prize is offered. Your interest is piqued. Juried shows are becoming more and more popular; judges are often internationally known. The competition is greater each year, the prizes are bigger, the publicity more rewarding.

This section is designed to help you avoid frustration, anger, or disappointment should you decide to enter a contest.

BE TRUE TO THE THEME

Be obvious in your quilt so that no one misses the connection between your treatment and the theme.

FOLLOW THE RULES EXACTLY

Consider every statement on the entry form highly significant, no matter how unimportant you think it might be. For example, if there are minimum and maximum measurements required, slavishly follow them. Wouldn't it be tragic if the finest quilt in the whole world were disqualified because it measured 1" (2.5 cm) too narrow?

DO YOUR HOMEWORK

Learn everything you can about the reputation of the show itself, about companies offering the prizes, and about the judges involved. Ask yourself some questions:

1. How big is the show? The bigger the show, the greater the prize money, and the keener the competition.

2. If it's a juried show, who makes up the jury?

3. If it's a judged show, who are the judges?

Romantica #19, p. 120

Romantica #20, p. 124

Romantica #21, p. 128

4. What are their likes and dislikes? Personal tastes? Prejudices?

5. Who has won awards at past shows? For what kind of quilts?

6. What product does the company sponsor sell? If there is space on the entry blank, indicate that you used their product (if you did).

Remember, companies are looking for good advertising material while judges are looking for ways to eliminate quilts. You may want to make a quilt that will fit a particular company's expectations or a specific judge's taste. Of course, it's okay to enter for the sole purpose of getting critiqued.

CHECK YOUR QUILT

Pretending you are a judge, ask yourself the following questions:

1. Is the quilt squeaky clean (no pencil marks, fingerprints, blood, food stains, animal hair, or stale odors)?

2. Does the quilt have visual impact?

3. Is there color harmony? Balance?

4. Are the appliqué stitches fine with no puckering? Do any stitches show? Does the thread match the design fabric?

5. Are the circles symmetrical?

6. Are the points sharp?

7. Do any threads peek out?

8. Are the design pieces on grain with the background? If not, write an explanation on your entry form: "The pieces are not on grain with the background fabric. This has been done on purpose for additional texture."

9. Is there sufficient quilting? Not enough quilting is a common complaint of judges. Are the stitches consistent, small, the same size on both sides? Is the marking visible? Are any knots showing? Are the straight lines of quilting evenly spaced? Does the quilting pattern compliment the design?

10. Is the binding straight, not wavy? Is it the same width all the way around, front and back? Square at the corners? No stitches showing? The joining true? The ending hidden? Does it relate to the quilt in terms of color, texture, and width?

11. Does the batting extend to the edge of the binding without lumping?

12. Is the quilt straight with no puckering, distortion, stretching, or waving? Check this out by hanging the quilt; don't just lay it out on a bed or on the floor. Usually a photo of your hanging quilt is a requirement for entry.

MAKE GOOD SLIDES

Often the entry form will give you some pointers on what makes a good photo and what kind of a photo is expected. Pay attention.

FILL OUT THE ENTRY FORM NEATLY AND COMPLETELY

The sample AQS entry form on the facing page is typical of what shows require.

MAILING

1. Be sure your quilt is labeled with a fabric label stitched to the back of the quilt that includes the name of the quilt, your name, address, and phone number.

2. Fold your quilt carefully and wrap it in acid free tissue paper. Place the wrapped quilt in a plastic bag to protect it against dampness. Also, cover the quilt with a sheet of cardboard for protection when box is cut open.

3. Pack it in a strong box. Label the destination and the source clearly.

4. The size of the box should be adequate to hold the quilt, not so small you have to wad up the quilt or so large that the box could be smashed during shipping.

5. Enclose a self-addressed stamped postcard for acknowledgment of receipt of the quilt. Type or print on the reverse side: the name of the quilt, your name, date received, signature, and position of the person signing for the quilt.

6. Insure the package.

AQS Quilt Contest
Entry Blank To Accompany Slides (may be photocopied)

Membership # _____
Name(s) _____
(Please Print)   List additional names on back of entry form.
Street _____
City _____ State ___ Zip _____
Phone (____)_____
Fax (____)_____
Local Newspaper _____
Circle **One** Category Number:(See rules 9, 10, & 11 for size)
Original Design: ☐ Yes   ☐ No
Quilted by: ☐ Hand   ☐ Machine
Quilt Title _____
Quilt Size (inches) _____
Basic Techniques _____
_____
Brief Description of Quilt for Show Booklet _____
_____
_____
_____

Approximate Insurance Value $ _____
(Over $1,000 requires a written appraisal; Maximum $5,000.00)
I wish to enter the above item and agree to abide by the quilt contest rules & decisions of the jury and judges. I understand that AQS will take every precaution to protect my quilt exhibited in this show. I realize they cannot be responsible for the acts of nature beyond their control. You may have my permission to photograph this quilt. If my quilt is exhibited in the American Quilter's Society Show, I understand that my signature gives AQS the right to use a photo of my quilt in any publications, advertisements, or promotional materials.

Signature _____

Social Security # _____
Please put your name on the slide mounts & mail slides, entry blank, and fee for each quilt (AQS members, $4.00; nonmembers, $25.00) to: **American Quilter's Society**, Klaudeen Hansen, P.O. Box 3290, Dept. Entry, Paducah, KY 42002-3290.

OTHER COMMENTS

Under no circumstances copy an original design and claim it as your design. If it is copyrighted, this is illegal. If you change some aspect of the design, you can say "this is an adaptation of..." or "this was inspired by..." and give the person's name and the name of the design. Giving credit to the designer does not diminish your creation.

Unfortunately, you need to be aware of some negatives regarding quilt competitions. In many shows, team quilts (for example, one person appliqués and another quilts) and group quilts (a number of people do the top and quilting) are lumped together, which is often a disadvantage. Some judges look for original designs only. An exquisitely executed quilt may be passed over if it is noticeable that it has been done from a workshop or a popular book.

Always enter a contest with the expectation of winning. However, if you do not win, you still reap the benefit of having the judges' critiques. Therefore, do not hesitate to enter.

A ribbon mentality is easy to acquire. Winning feels so good. Viewers respond with compliments. Writers seek you out for articles. Magazines ask to picture your creation on their covers. Quiltmakers recognize you and your work. Prizes are fun to receive. A money award is intoxicating. Your home gets decorated with what amounts to a quilter's loving cup and you get to show off your ribbons and other awards with pride to family, friends, and casual visitors. If you aren't interested in seeking awards, you can bask in the sunshine of praise from everyone who sees your magnificent treasure. Take the challenge!

Block Patterns

Exotica
Block designs #1–#9

 The Best of Jacobean Appliqué   Patricia B. Campbell and Mimi Ayars

Romantica
Block designs #10–#21

DESIGN # 1
upper left quadrant

13

15R

15

14

16

17

5

7

DESIGN # 1
upper right quadrant

Numbers on pattern pieces in each design are for identification, not stitching order.

Add turn-under allowances when cutting fabric pieces.

DESIGN # 1
lower left quadrant

7

12

6

8

9

Numbers on pattern pieces in
each design are for identification,
not stitching order.

Add turn-under
allowances when cutting
fabric pieces.

1

DESIGN # 1
lower right quadrant

Block Patterns

DESIGN # 2
upper left quadrant

21

19

17

20

16

8   7   2

DESIGN # 2
upper right quadrant

Numbers on pattern pieces in
each design are for identification,
not stitching order.

Add turn-under
allowances when cutting
fabric pieces.

DESIGN # 2
lower left quadrant

The Best of Jacobean Appliqué ❧ Patricia B. Campbell and Mimi Ayars

Numbers on pattern pieces in
each design are for identification,
not stitching order.

Add turn-under
allowances when cutting
fabric pieces.

2

4

3

1

DESIGN # 2
lower right quadrant

DESIGN # 3
upper left quadrant

DESIGN # 3
upper right quadrant

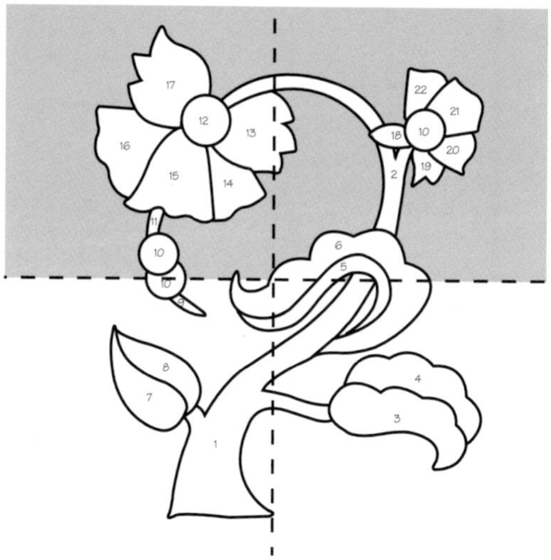

22

21

13

10

18

20

19

2

Numbers on pattern pieces in
each design are for identification,
not stitching order.

Add turn-under
allowances when cutting
fabric pieces.

6

5

1

Numbers on pattern pieces in
each design are for identification,
not stitching order.

Add turn-under
allowances when cutting
fabric pieces.

DESIGN # 3
lower left quadrant

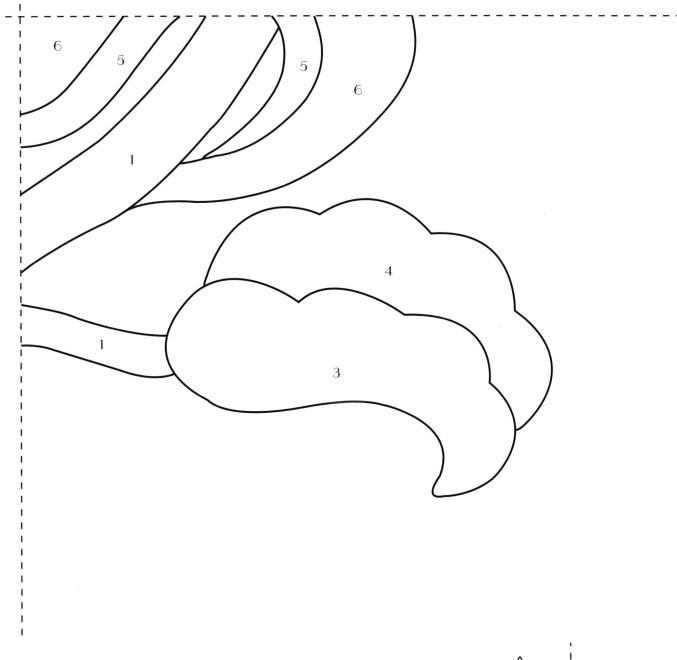

6

5

5

6

1

4

1

3

DESIGN # 3
lower right quadrant

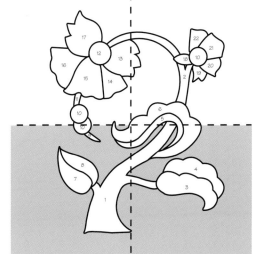

DESIGN # 4
upper left quadrant

Numbers on pattern pieces in
each design are for identification,
not stitching order.

Add turn-under
allowances when cutting
fabric pieces.

The Best of Jacobean Appliqué ❧ Patricia B. Campbell and Mimi Ayars

DESIGN # 4
upper right quadrant

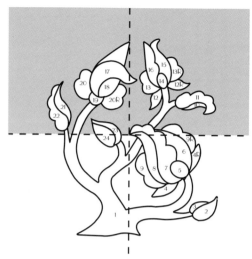

17

15

16

13R

14

13

12R

12

11

10

9R

8   7   6

Numbers on pattern pieces in
each design are for identification,
not stitching order.

Add turn-under
allowances when cutting
fabric pieces.

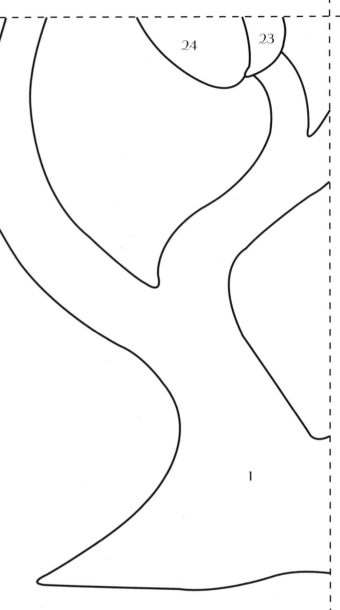

24   23

I

DESIGN # 4
lower left quadrant

DESIGN # 4
lower right quadrant

Block Patterns

Tulip template pattern
on p. 136.

DESIGN # 5
upper left quadrant

2

9

7

8R

3

6R

6

6R

6R

6R

6

2

3

The Best of Jacobean Appliqué ✤ Patricia B. Campbell and Mimi Ayars

DESIGN # 5
upper right quadrant

Numbers on pattern pieces in
each design are for identification,
not stitching order.

Add turn-under
allowances when cutting
fabric pieces.

7

8R

3R

3

6

6

6

6

2

5

4

6R

6R

1

6R

6R

6R

6

6

3

6

6

10   11

6

6

9

9

1

DESIGN # 5
lower left quadrant

1

6R

6R

9

8

7

9

5

4

Numbers on pattern pieces in
each design are for identification,
not stitching order.

Add turn-under
allowances when cutting
fabric pieces.

Tulip template pattern
on p. 136.

DESIGN # 5
lower right quadrant

DESIGN # 6
upper left quadrant

DESIGN # 6
upper right quadrant

Numbers on pattern pieces in
each design are for identification,
not stitching order.

Add turn-under
allowances when cutting
fabric pieces.

Numbers on pattern pieces in
each design are for identification,
not stitching order.

Add turn-under
allowances when cutting
fabric pieces.

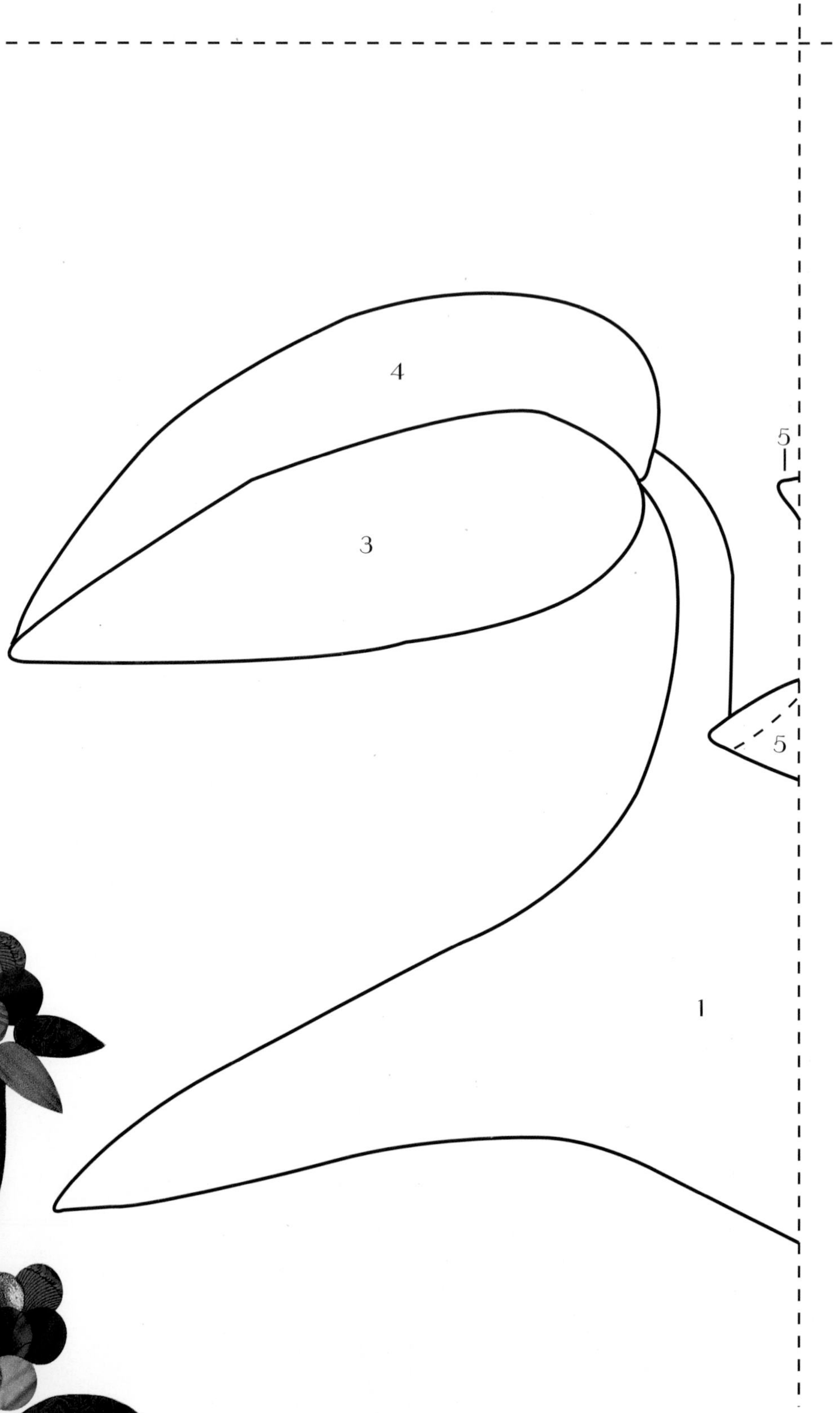

4

3

5

5

1

2

DESIGN # 6
lower left quadrant

DESIGN # 6
lower right quadrant

DESIGN # 7
upper left quadrant

18R

17

22

16

21

19R

15

20

16R

17R

19

18

12

Numbers on pattern pieces in
each design are for identification,
not stitching order.

12

10

Add turn-under
allowances when cutting
fabric pieces.

11

9

8

DESIGN # 7
upper right quadrant

22

13

14   6

11

12

10R

12R

9R

5

4

8

3

2

1

DESIGN # 7
lower left quadrant

The Best of Jacobean Appliqué ⁂ Patricia B. Campbell and Mimi Ayars

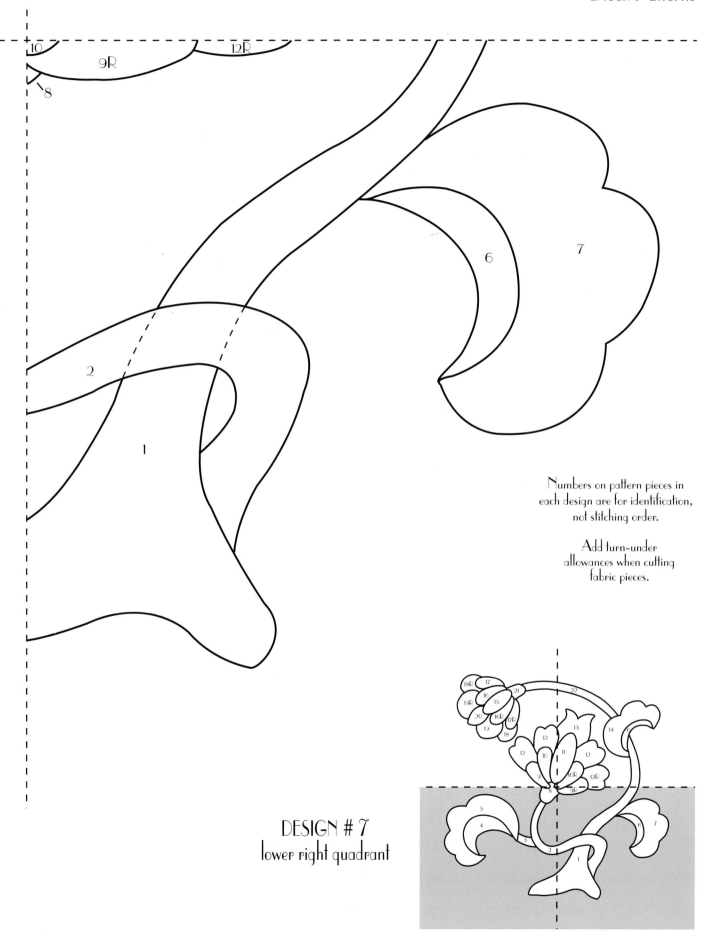

10
9R
12R
8
6
7
2
1

Numbers on pattern pieces in
each design are for identification,
not stitching order.

Add turn-under
allowances when cutting
fabric pieces.

DESIGN # 7
lower right quadrant

Block Patterns

DESIGN # 8
upper left quadrant

22

21

23

9

25

15

15

15

10

12

14

15

11

8

15

15   13

The Best of Jacobean Appliqué ⚘ Patricia B. Campbell and Mimi Ayars

DESIGN # 8
upper right quadrant

Numbers on pattern pieces in
each design are for identification,
not stitching order.

Add turn-under
allowances when cutting
fabric pieces.

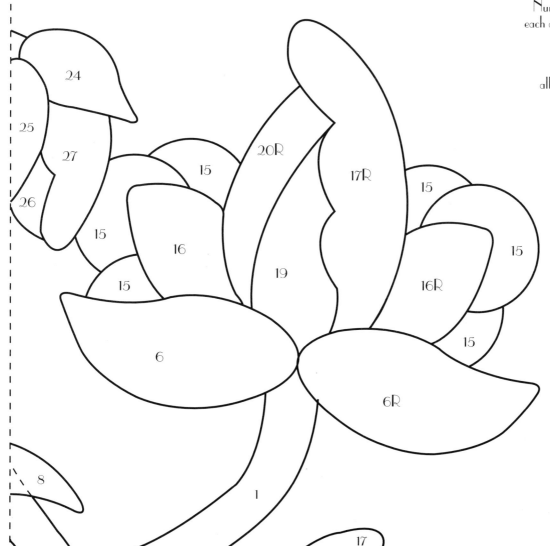

DESIGN # 8
lower left quadrant

9

15   15   17

15   16   19   20   15

15   16R   15

6R   18   16R   15

6   15

5

1

Numbers on pattern pieces in
each design are for identification,
not stitching order.

Add turn-under
allowances when cutting
fabric pieces.

DESIGN # 8
lower right quadrant

Block Patterns

DESIGN # 9
upper left quadrant

16

13

14

15

3

12

11

2

10

DESIGN # 9
upper right quadrant

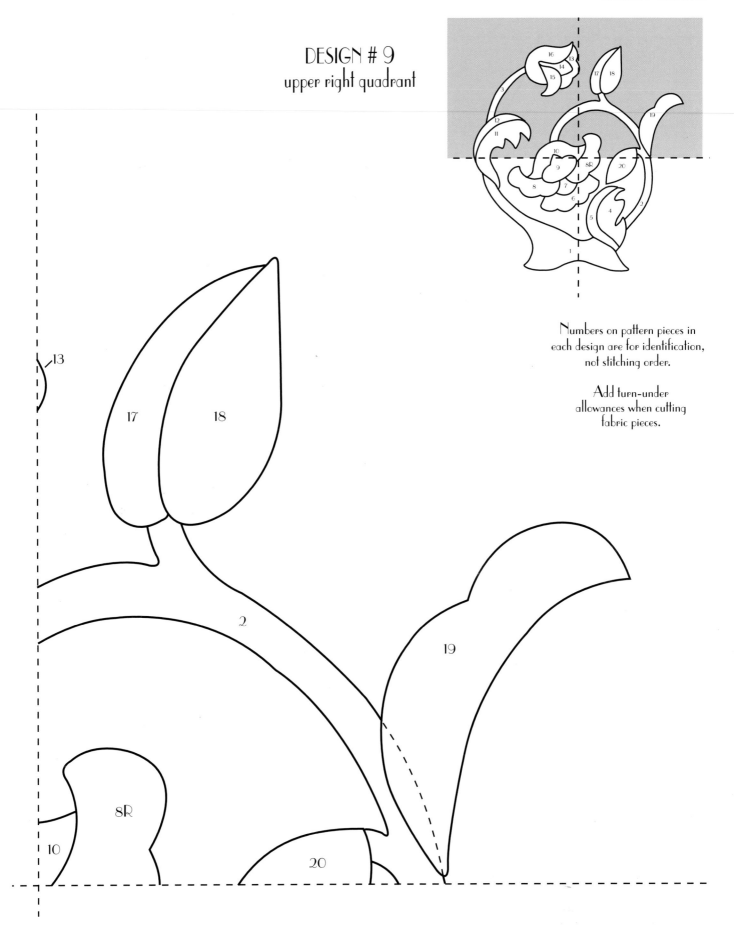

Numbers on pattern pieces in
each design are for identification,
not stitching order.

Add turn-under
allowances when cutting
fabric pieces.

13

17   18

2

19

8R

10

20

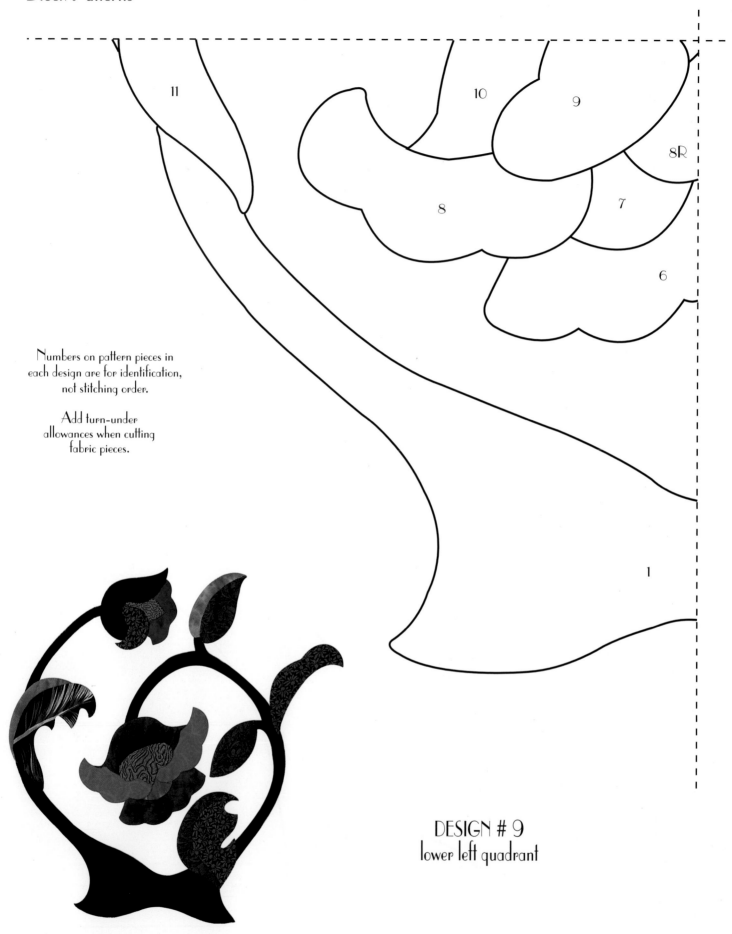

11

10

9

8R

8

7

6

Numbers on pattern pieces in
each design are for identification,
not stitching order.

Add turn-under
allowances when cutting
fabric pieces.

1

DESIGN # 9
lower left quadrant

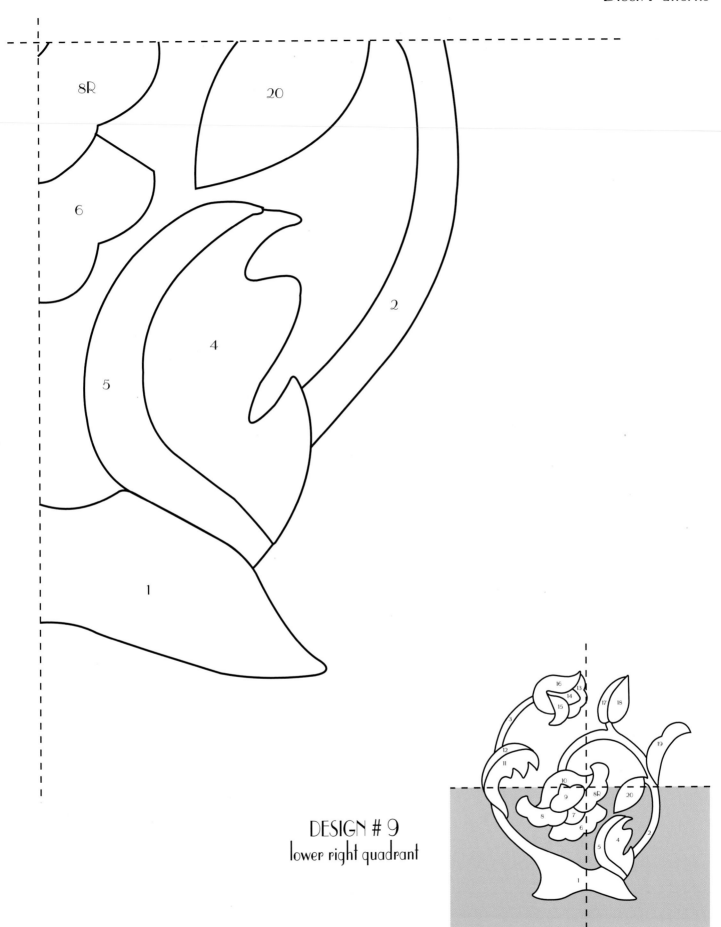

8R

20

6

2

4

5

1

DESIGN # 9
lower right quadrant

DESIGN # 10
upper left quadrant

Numbers on pattern pieces in
each design are for identification,
not stitching order.

Add turn-under
allowances when cutting
fabric pieces.

Sample for "under" and "over"
stitching. See pages 28-29 for
explanation of arrows.

bias

25

24

23

21

22

21

26

21

17

14

20

18   19

14

bias

DESIGN # 10
upper right quadrant

bias

36
31
27
32
30
29
28
33
34
35
bias
10

DESIGN # 10
lower left quadrant

10

bias

9

12

8

7

6

11

2

4

5

1

Numbers on pattern pieces in each design are for identification, not stitching order.

Add turn-under allowances when cutting fabric pieces.

Sample for "under" and "over" stitching. See pages 28-29 for explanation of arrows.

DESIGN # 10
lower right quadrant

DESIGN # 11
upper left quadrant

Numbers on pattern pieces in
each design are for identification, not stitching order.

Add turn-under
allowances when cutting
fabric pieces.

1

1

1

2

3

4

2R

13

15

12

14

9

18

16

Block Patterns

DESIGN # 11
upper right quadrant

12

16

27R

9

27

9

Numbers on pattern pieces in
each design are for identification,
not stitching order.

Add turn-under
allowances when cutting
fabric pieces.

26

17

DESIGN # 11
lower left quadrant

The Best of Jacobean Appliqué ⚭ Patricia B. Campbell and Mimi Ayars

10

22

20

21

25

23

17

9

DESIGN # 11
lower right quadrant

DESIGN # 12
upper left quadrant

13

12

bias

bias

bias

1

1

1

Numbers on pattern pieces in
each design are for identification,
not stitching order.

Add turn-under
allowances when cutting
fabric pieces.

14

1

1

The Best of Jacobean Appliqué ❧ Patricia B. Campbell and Mimi Ayars

DESIGN # 12
upper right quadrant

bias

bias

1

7

8

1

1

1

1

10

10

9

9

9

bias

9

DESIGN # 12
lower left quadrant

 The Best of Jacobean Appliqué ❧ Patricia B. Campbell and Mimi Ayars

14

bias

16   9

15

11

Numbers on pattern pieces in
each design are for identification,
not stitching order.

Add turn-under
allowances when cutting
fabric pieces.

DESIGN # 12
lower right quadrant

DESIGN # 13
upper left quadrant

DESIGN # 13
upper right quadrant

12

12

bias

11

11

11

11

11

11

11

11

10

9

9R

6

8

Numbers on pattern pieces in
each design are for identification, not stitching order.

Add turn-under
allowances when cutting
fabric pieces.

12

12

6

11

11

11

11

11

11

11

11

11

11

9

9R

10

1

9

Numbers on pattern pieces in
each design are for identification, not stitching order.

Add turn-under
allowances when cutting
fabric pieces.

DESIGN # 13
lower left quadrant

9

9R

6

8

7

6

4

4

5

5

10

3

5

2

5

9R

4

5

4

1

DESIGN # 13
lower right quadrant

DESIGN # 14
upper left quadrant

Numbers on pattern pieces in
each design are for identification, not stitching order.

Add turn-under
allowances when cutting
fabric pieces.

Tulip template pattern on p. 136.

bias

27

28

29

30

31

26

25

20

20

20

20

20

20

21

24

23

DESIGN # 14
upper right quadrant

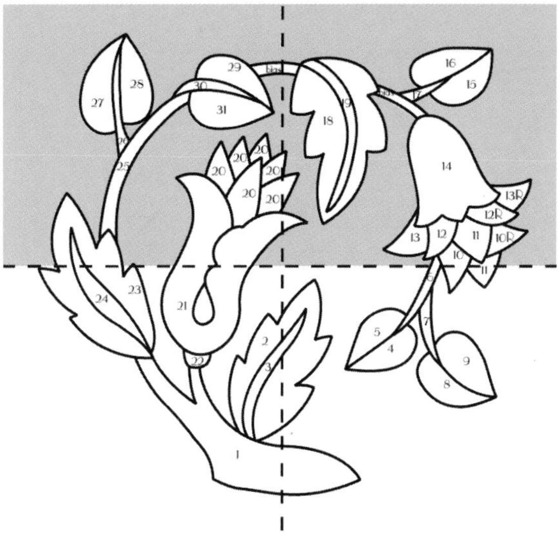

bias

16

15

17

bias

19

18

14

20

20

13R

12R

21

13

12

11

10R

6

10

11

Numbers on pattern pieces in
each design are for identification, not stitching order.

Add turn-under
allowances when cutting
fabric pieces.

Tulip template pattern on p. 136.

24

23

21

22

2

3

1

DESIGN # 14
lower left quadrant

DESIGN # 14
lower right quadrant

DESIGN # 15
upper left quadrant

DESIGN # 15
upper right quadrant

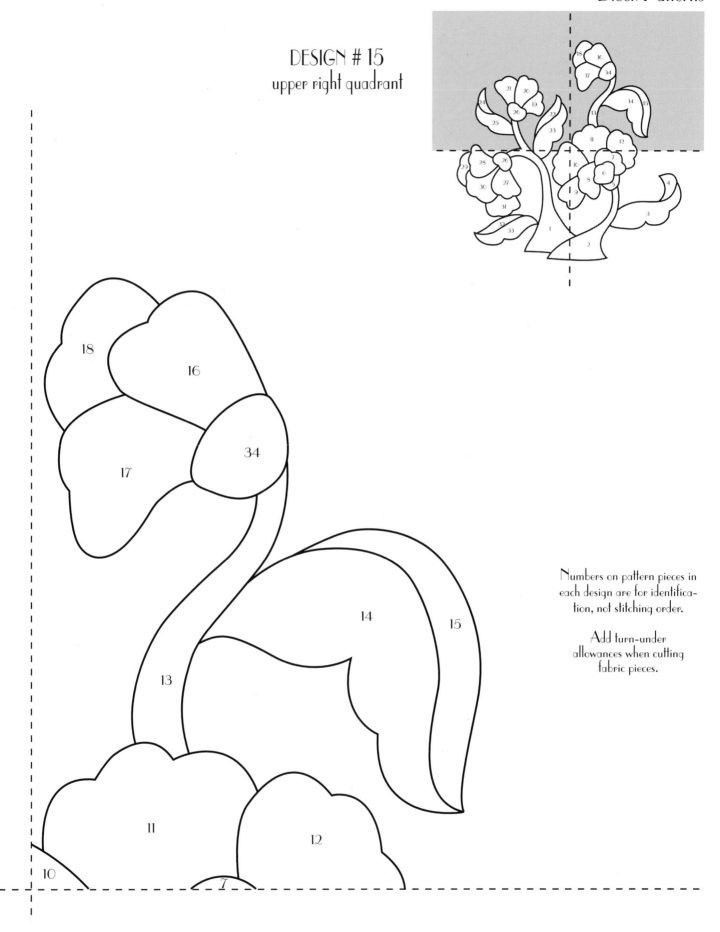

Numbers on pattern pieces in
each design are for identification, not stitching order.

Add turn-under
allowances when cutting
fabric pieces.

DESIGN # 15
lower left quadrant

11

7

12

10

6

8

4

9

5

3

1

Numbers on pattern shapes
indicate stitching order.

Add turn-under
allowances when cutting
fabric pieces.

2

DESIGN # 15
lower right quadrant

DESIGN # 16
upper left quadrant

Numbers on pattern pieces in
each design are for identification,
not for stitching order.

Add turn-under
allowances when cutting
fabric pieces.

4

14

5

12

12

14R

12

12

12

23

12

4R

24

21

2

20

1

18

3

bias

18

DESIGN # 16
upper right quadrant

3

8

7

19

10

16

14R

4R

5

17

17

17

13

15R

6R

18

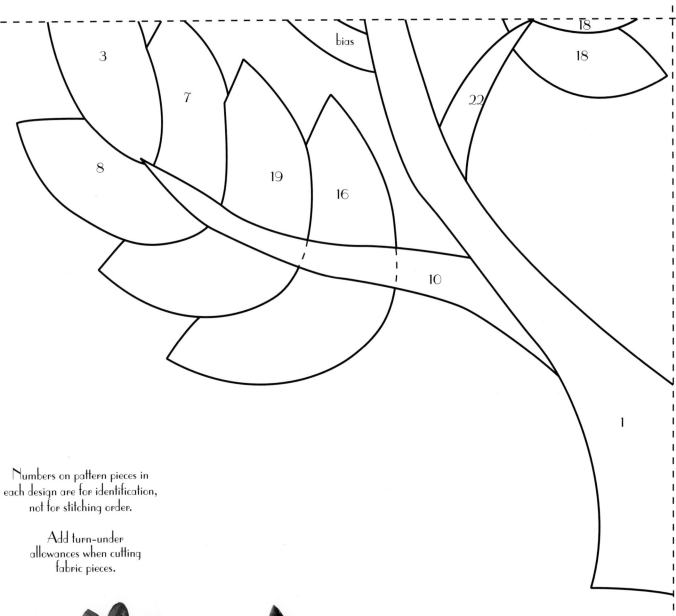

3

7

8

bias

18
18

22

19

16

10

1

Numbers on pattern pieces in
each design are for identification,
not for stitching order.

Add turn-under
allowances when cutting
fabric pieces.

DESIGN # 16
lower left quadrant

17
13
15R
6R
12
15
12
12
6
12
12
12
2
9
22
9
9
1
20

DESIGN # 16
lower right quadrant

Block Patterns

DESIGN # 17
upper left quadrant

Numbers on pattern pieces in
each design are for identification,
not for stitching order.

Add turn-under
allowances when cutting
fabric pieces.

22

21

24

1

25

26

16

27

33

32

28

17

29

31

30

DESIGN # 17
upper right quadrant

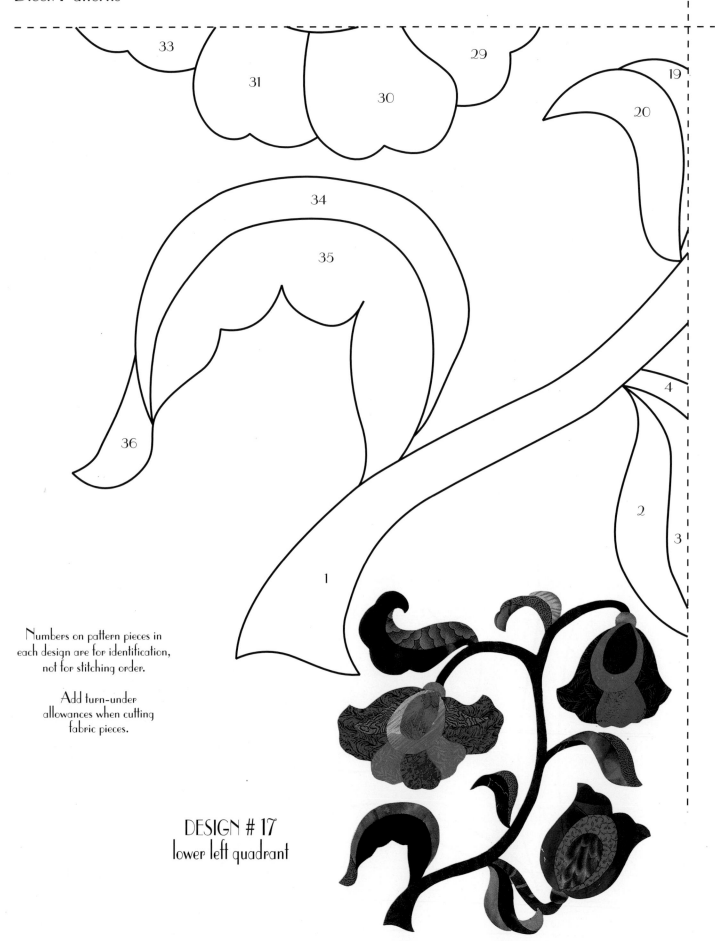

33

31

29

30

19

20

34

35

36

4

2

3

1

Numbers on pattern pieces in
each design are for identification,
not for stitching order.

Add turn-under
allowances when cutting
fabric pieces.

DESIGN # 17
lower left quadrant

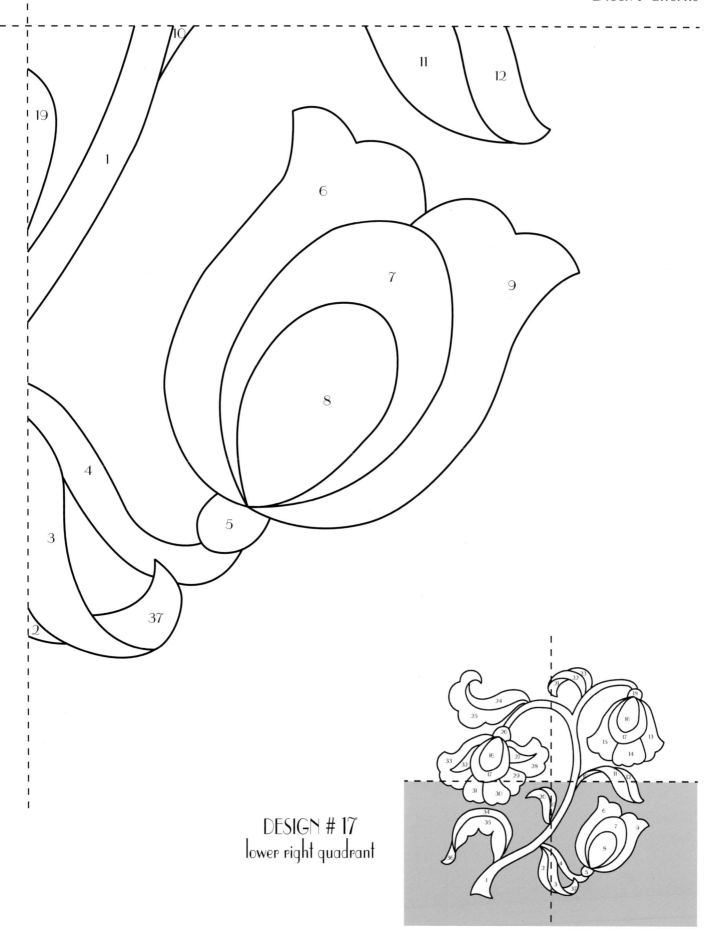

DESIGN # 17
lower right quadrant

Block Patterns

DESIGN # 18
upper left quadrant

30

31

32

30

27

25   25

29   30

25

26

28

1

23

24

19

18   14

15

DESIGN # 18
upper right quadrant

Numbers on pattern pieces in
each design are for identification, not for stitching order.

Add turn-under
allowances when cutting
fabric pieces.

24

23

19

18

14

15

22

22

bias

22

21

20

1

2

DESIGN # 18
lower left quadrant

14

13

27

15

12

4

3

1

2

Numbers on pattern pieces in
each design are for identification, not for stitching order.

Add turn-under
allowances when cutting
fabric pieces.

DESIGN # 18
lower right quadrant

DESIGN # 19
upper left quadrant

Numbers on pattern pieces in
each design are for identification, not stitching order.

Add turn-under
allowances when cutting
fabric pieces.

35

34

36

1

33

26

32

27

31

29

28

19

30

20

25

21

DESIGN # 19
upper right quadrant

25

21

22

39

24

6

23

5

Numbers on pattern pieces in
each design are for identification, not stitching order.

Add turn-under
allowances when cutting
fabric pieces.

1

DESIGN # 19
lower left quadrant

DESIGN # 19
lower right quadrant

DESIGN # 20
upper left quadrant

DESIGN # 20
upper right quadrant

−21

−18

29

30

29R

28

28R

27

26

25

bias

Numbers on pattern pieces in
each design are for identification, not stitching order.

Add turn-under
allowances when cutting
fabric pieces.

21

22

20

23   17R   17   18

15

7

6

6   7

23

5

4

11

10

2

3

1

DESIGN # 20
lower left quadrant

23

18

17R   20   17

16R   16   15

24   19   14

11

10   13

1

12

Numbers on pattern pieces in
each design are for identification,
not stitching order.

Add turn-under
allowances when cutting
fabric pieces.

DESIGN # 20
lower right quadrant

DESIGN # 21
upper left quadrant

DESIGN # 21
upper right quadrant

Numbers on pattern pieces in
each design are for identification,
not stitching order.

Add turn-under
allowances when cutting
fabric pieces.

DESIGN # 21
lower left quadrant

The Best of Jacobean Appliqué ❧ Patricia B. Campbell and Mimi Ayars

16

12

13

10

11

14

4

15

9

3

14

8

7

2

6

1

Numbers on pattern pieces in
each design are for identification,
not stitching order.

Add turn-under
allowances when cutting
fabric pieces.

DESIGN # 21
lower right quadrant

Border Patterns

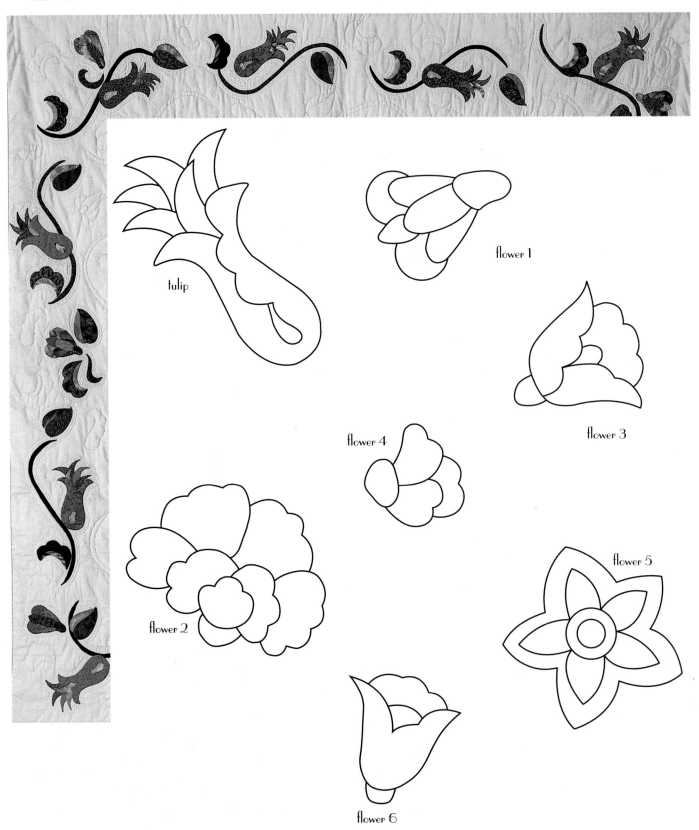

tulip

flower 1

flower 3

flower 4

flower 2

flower 5

flower 6

The Best of Jacobean Appliqué ☙ Patricia B. Campbell and Mimi Ayars

leaf 1

leaf 2

leaf 4

leaf 3

single leaves

swirl 1

swirl 3

swirl 4

swirl 2

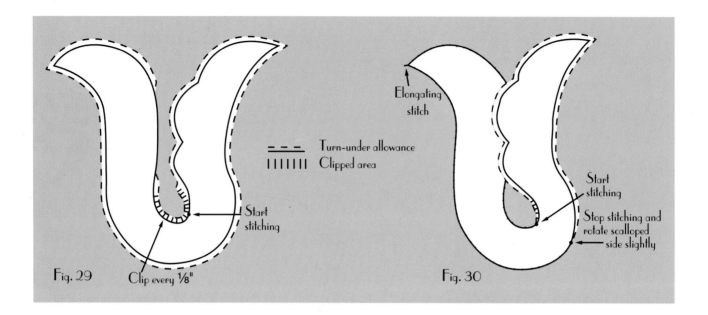

Fig. 29   Clip every ⅛"

- - -   Turn-under allowance
|||||| Clipped area

Start stitching

Elongating stitch

Start stitching

Stop stitching and rotate scalloped side slightly

Fig. 30

Place the template on as much design fabric bias as possible. (Left-handers: flip the tulip template when placing it on the design fabric. Then the non-scalloped side will be on the right, ready for you to stitch clockwise.) Cut out, leaving the turn-under allowance on the scalloped side (Fig. 29); this will overlap the straight side (Fig. 30). There is no hump at the fabric base of the tulip when you stitch, as you might expect, because the side is pivoted only slightly. A tulip piece will let you show off your skill in stitching a "U," several "Vs," and two perfect points.

1. Stitch the tulip tips in place.

2. Clip the "U" at the inside bottom of the tulip evenly every ⅛" (.3 cm) (Fig. 29).

3. Pin the side that has the straight inside edge. Put pins on the back, so they are out of the way.

4. Start stitching as indicated on Fig. 29.

5. Continue stitching around the straight side until you're opposite your starting point (Fig. 30).

6. Move the scalloped side over the stitched side just enough to cover the place where there is no turn-under allowance. Pin in place, on the back.

7. Complete the stitching to your starting point.

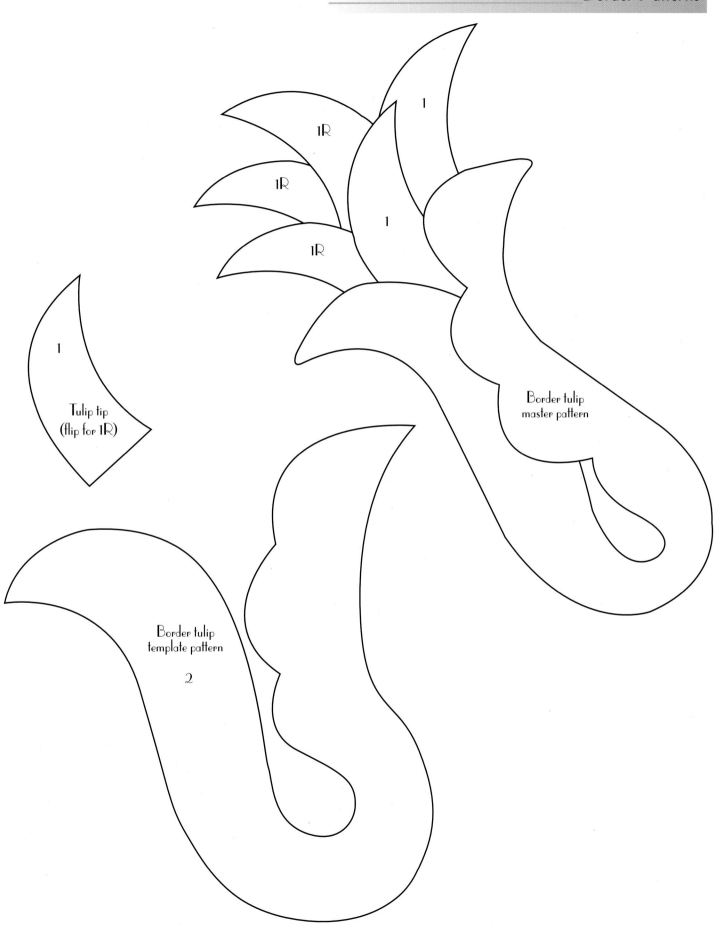

1

1R

1R

1R

1

1

1

Tulip tip
(flip for 1R)

Border tulip
master pattern

Border tulip
template pattern

2

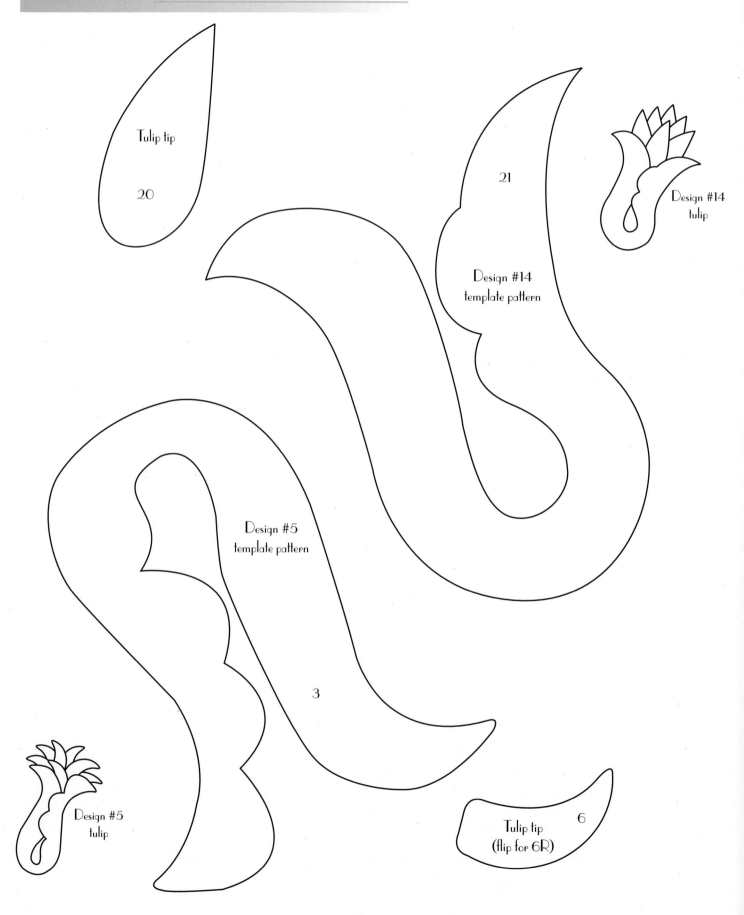

Tulip tip

20

21

Design #14
template pattern

Design #14
tulip

Design #5
template pattern

3

Design #5
tulip

Tulip tip
(flip for 6R)

6

flower 1

Choose stem patterns from pp. 140-141. Design your own or omit stems.

flower 2

flower 3

Use in any position, including reverse.

Choose stem patterns from pp. 140-141. Design your own or omit stems.

flower 5

flower 6

flower 4

Use in any position, including reverse.

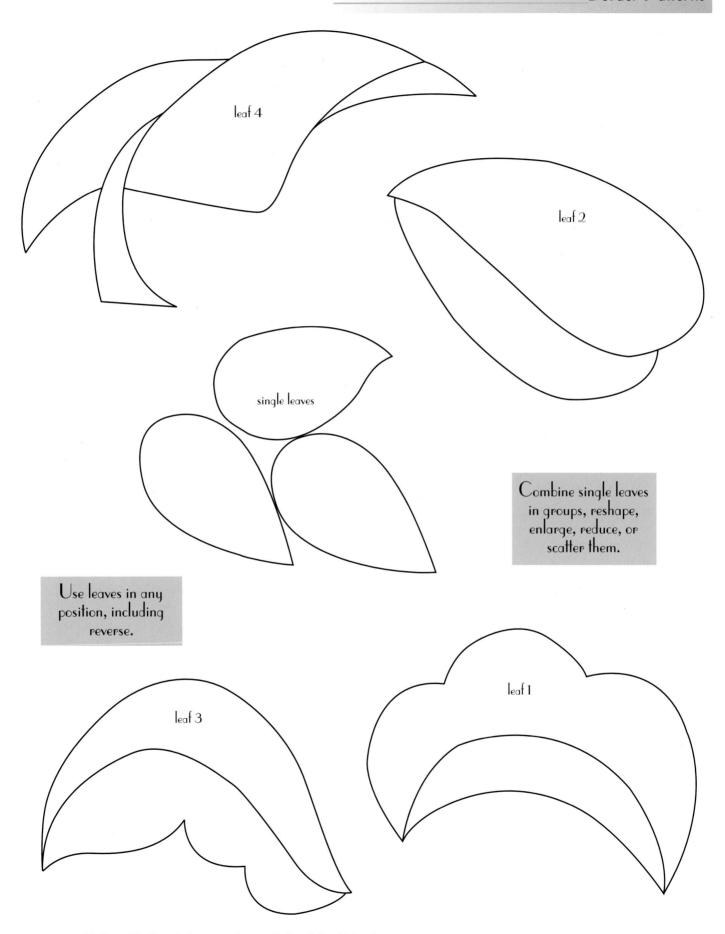

leaf 4

leaf 2

single leaves

Combine single leaves
in groups, reshape,
enlarge, reduce, or
scatter them.

Use leaves in any
position, including
reverse.

leaf 3

leaf 1

stem

stem

stem

stem

stem

stem

vine

vine

stem

stem

The Best of Jacobean Appliqué ❧ Patricia B. Campbell and Mimi Ayars

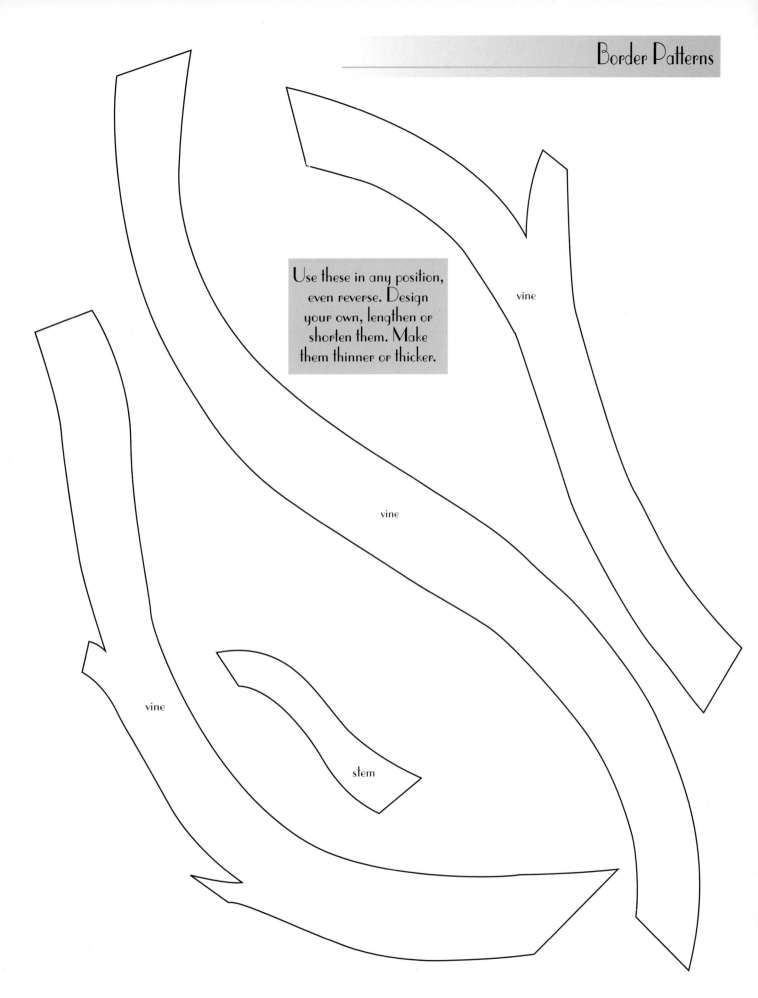

Use these in any position, even reverse. Design your own, lengthen or shorten them. Make them thinner or thicker.

vine

vine

vine

stem

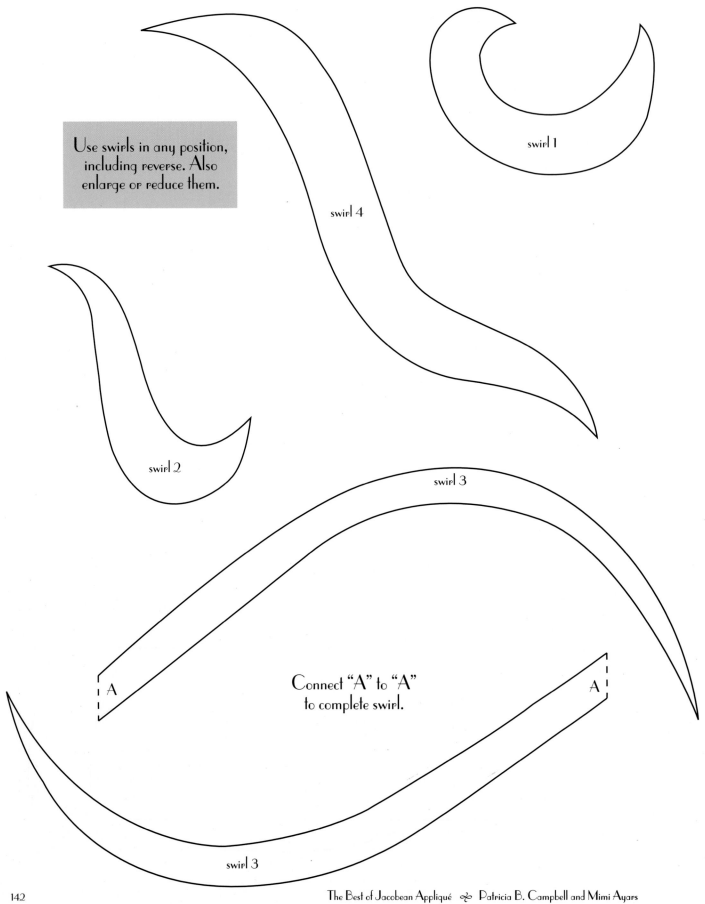

Use swirls in any position, including reverse. Also enlarge or reduce them.

swirl 1

swirl 4

swirl 2

swirl 3

A

Connect "A" to "A" to complete swirl.

A

swirl 3

The Authors

Patricia B. Campbell, born and reared in Michigan, makes her home in Dallas, Texas. An award-winning appliqué artist, she is well-known as an exciting speaker and an inspiring instructor. She has adapted seventeenth and eighteenth century Jacobean designs from embroidery to fabric and has created a line of patterns for sale. She also has a collection of fabrics, *Impressions* and *Fossil Fern*, manufactured by Benartex.

She has taught workshops from Maine to South Africa. Her first quilt, *Jacobean Arbor*, the well-known and beloved black quilt, won eight ribbons, including a Best of Show. It was followed by *Elizabethan Woods*, a five-time ribbon winner. She and her quilts have appeared on the covers of and been featured in articles in *American Quilter, International Quilt Festival, Quilting Today, Patchwork Quilt Tsuchin,* and *Quilting International*.

A native of Delaware, Mimi Ayars, Ph.D., calls herself a *hardy Texas transplant*. She caught the spirit of quilting in the 1976 revival while living in the Chicago area, once belonging to five guilds concurrently. Her first quilt, *Stars and Stripes*, was selected for a show of bicentennial quilts at the Museum of the American Quilter's Society in 1991.

Dr. Ayars has taught sociology at nine universities in six states. She retired in 1991 to pursue two hobbies: writing and quilting. Her articles on quilt making have been published in the *National Quilting Association's Quilting Quarterly* (formerly *Patchwork Patter*), and *Quilt World*.

She and Pat have published five books: *Jacobean Appliqué: Book I – "Exotica"* and *Jacobean Appliqué: Book II – "Romantica,"* AQS, 1993 and 1995; *Theorem Appliqué: Book I – Abundant Harvest* and *Theorem Appliqué: Book II – Summer Splendor,* Chitra, 1994 and 1995; *Jacobean Rhapsodies: Composing with 28 Appliqué Designs,* C&T, 1998.

They wrote this book as a guide. There are suggestions, hints, and advice; there is no *must*, no *have to*, no *only way*. The *right way* is your way. A freedom from precision exists with appliqué, unlike piecework. Enjoy that freedom. It's suggested that you follow the book's instructions for a trial period; if you don't like them, try another method or improvise.

Pat, as your tutor, shares her *tricks* and epiphanies (*ah-ha's*) to guide you. Mimi explains these with simplicity and clarity, step by step. Her illustrations and Richard Walker's photographs are great graphic helps. Each design is shown with a color photograph, a down-sized diagram, and a full-size master pattern divided into quadrants.

Your Jacobean appliqué quilt is your creation. Have fun making it and take pride in showing it.

PRODUCT RESOURCES

FABRIC
Benartex – "Fossil Fern" and "Impressions", Alexander Henry, Hoffman, Skydyes

BATTING
Hobbs "Thermore", Hobbs "Polydown", Richard Hemmings, Fairfield

THREAD
Mettler #60 Machine Embroidery
MC #50 Machine Embroidery

SCISSORS
Fiskars 5" Point, Gingher 4" Embroidery

NEEDLES
Clover #10 Betweens

PENCILS
Berol Prisma Color, Very Thin

PENS
Sharpie, Pigma

ERASER
Pentel Clic

QUILT FRAME
The Flynn Quilt Frame, Morgan Craft Stand

LAMP
Ott

Neither the authors nor AQS represent any of the companies who make the products suggested. The recommended items, however, have been tested by the authors and found to be consistently of high quality and reliability.

This is only a small selection of the books available from the American Quilter's Society. AQS books are known worldwide for timely topics, clear writing, beautiful color photos, and accurate illustrations and patterns. The following books are available from your local bookseller, quilt shop, or public library.

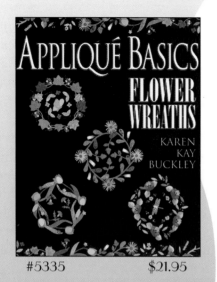

#5335 $21.95

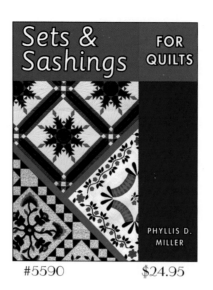

#5590 $24.95

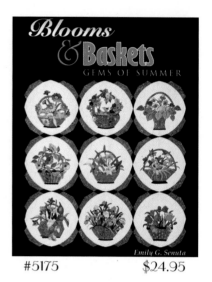

#5175 $24.95

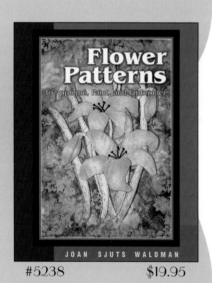

#5238 $19.95

#5591 $19.95

#5013 $14.95

5336 $22.95

#4833 $14.95

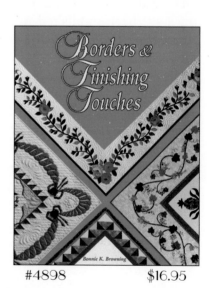

#4898 $16.95

LOOK FOR THESE BOOKS NATIONALLY OR CALL 1-800-626-5420